THE PICTURE BOOK OF
SUNSETS

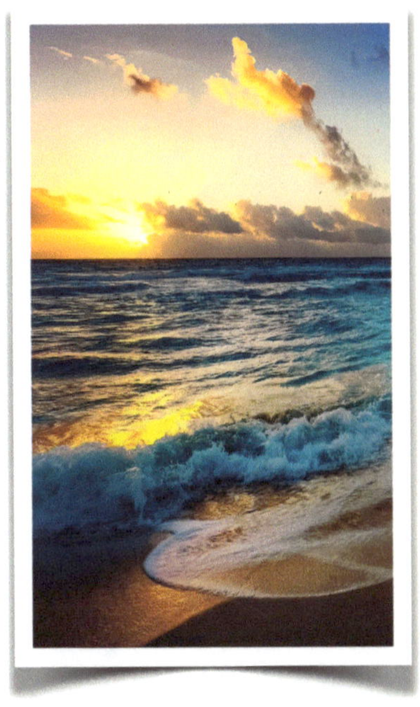

SUNNY STREET
BOOKS

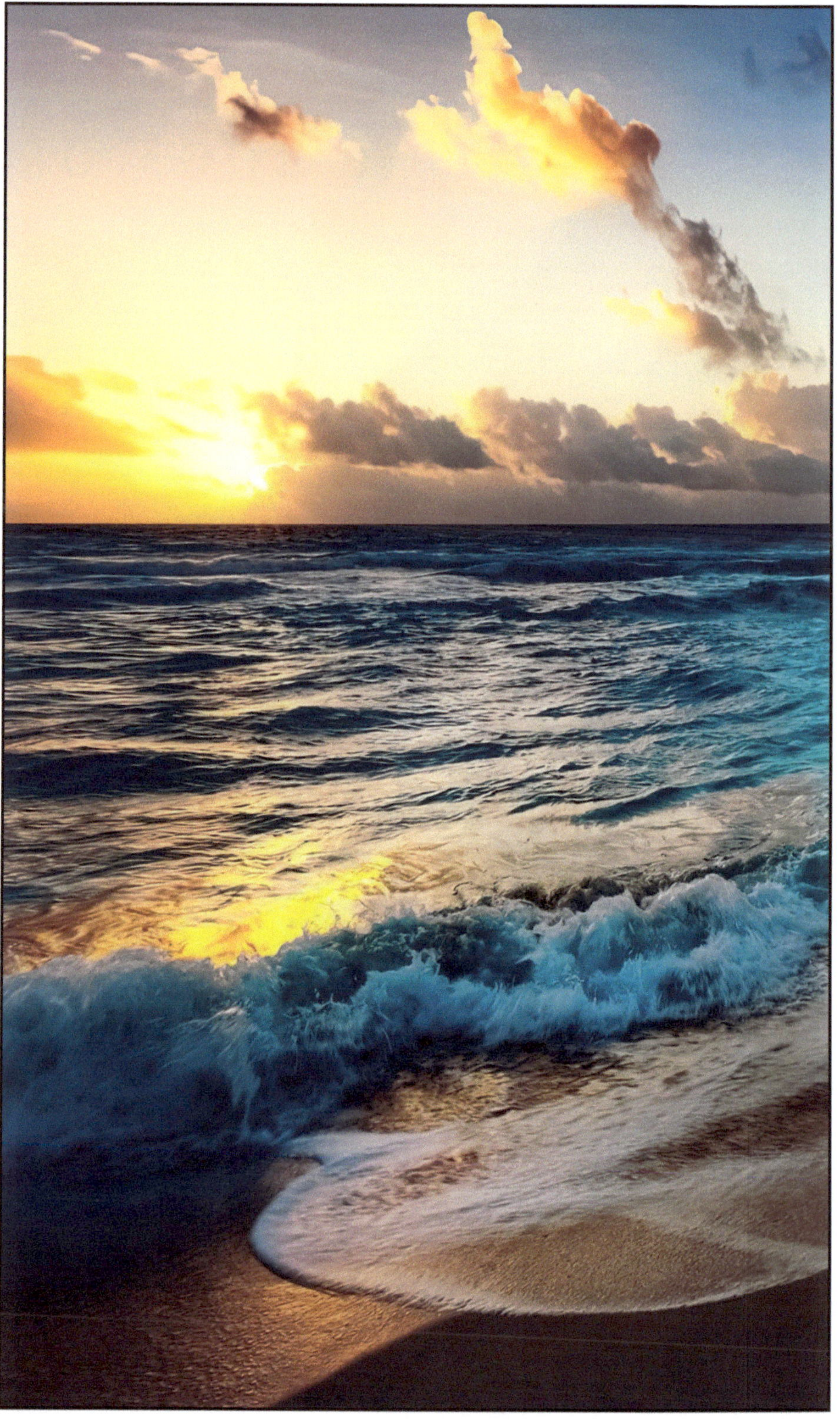

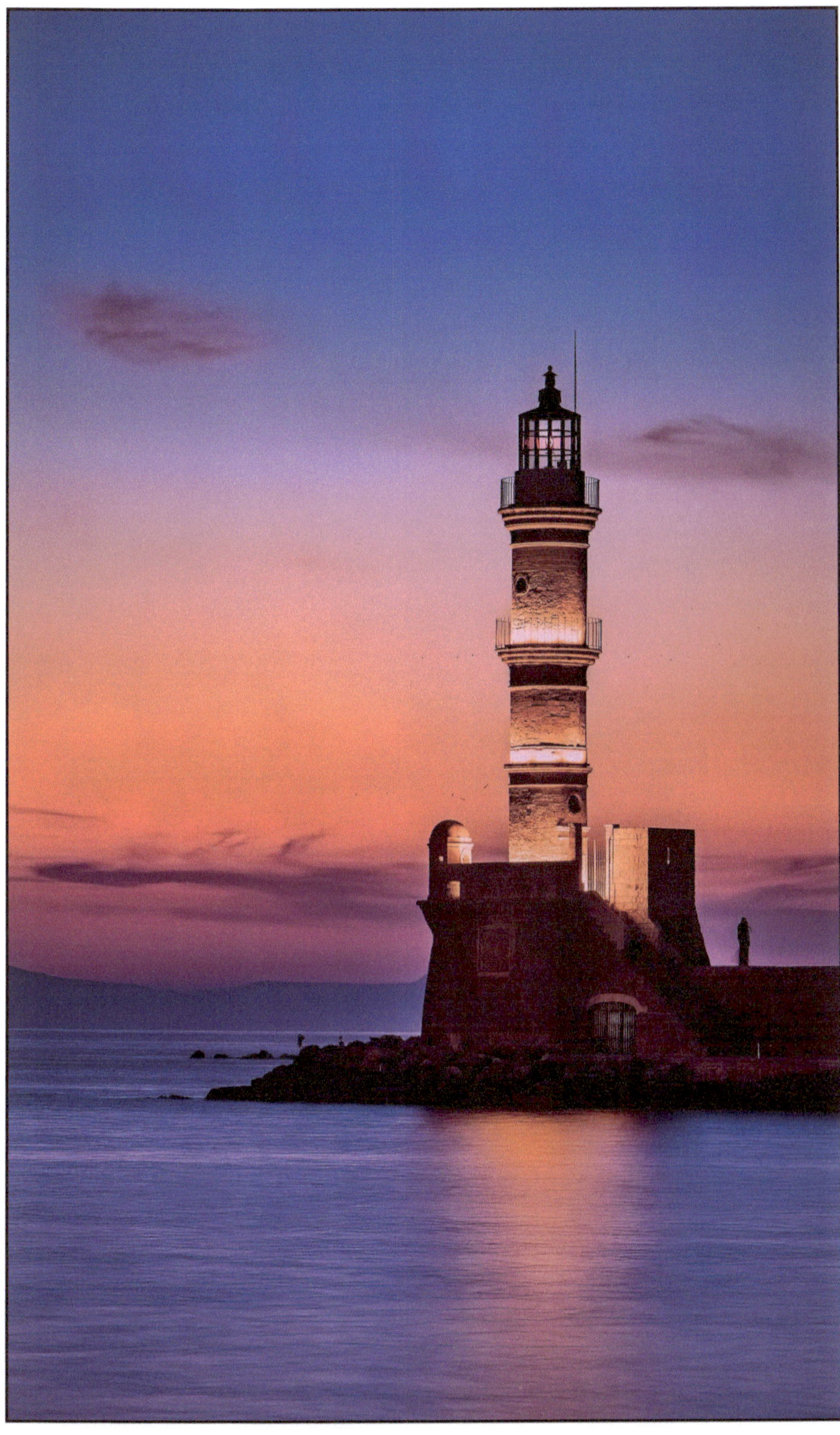

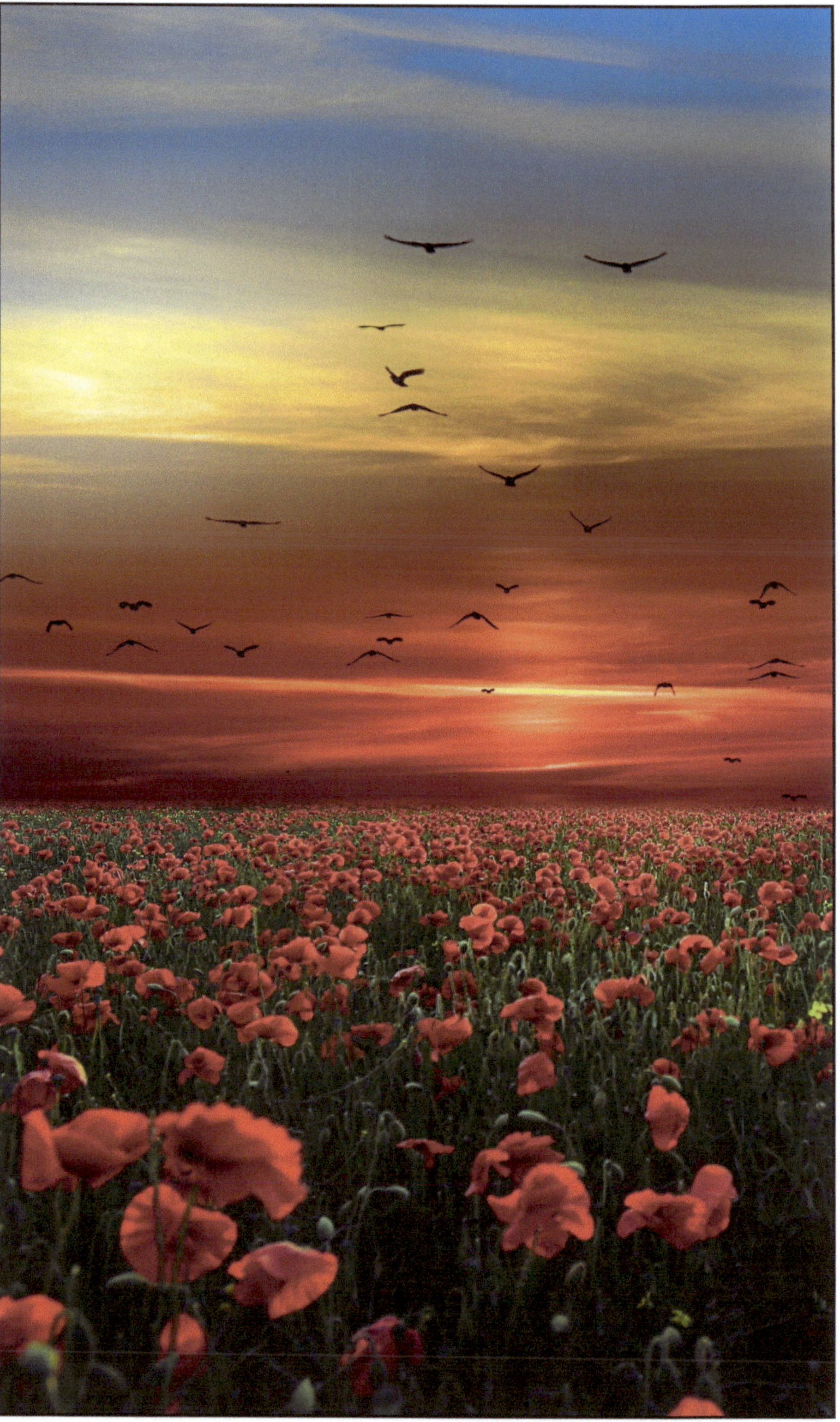

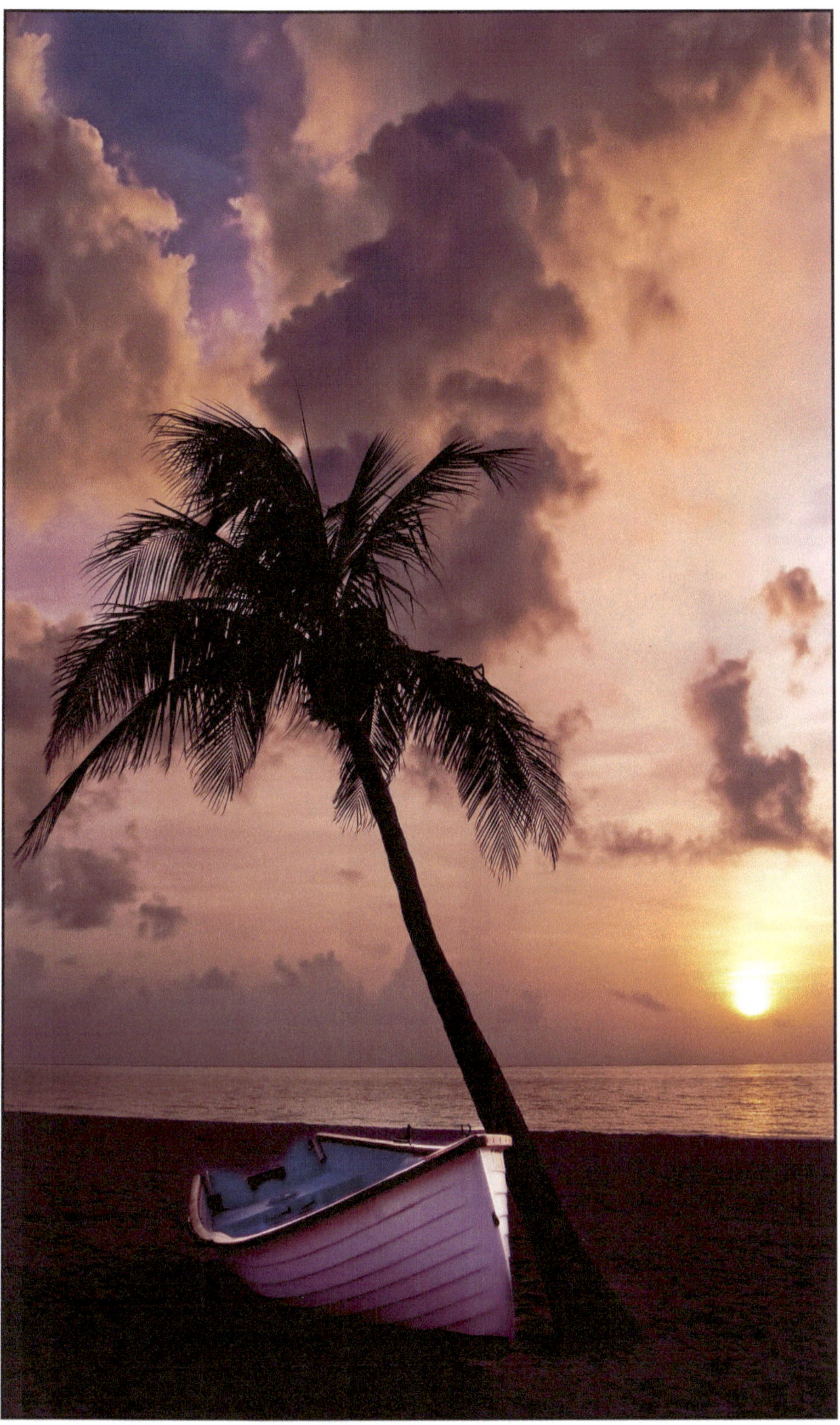

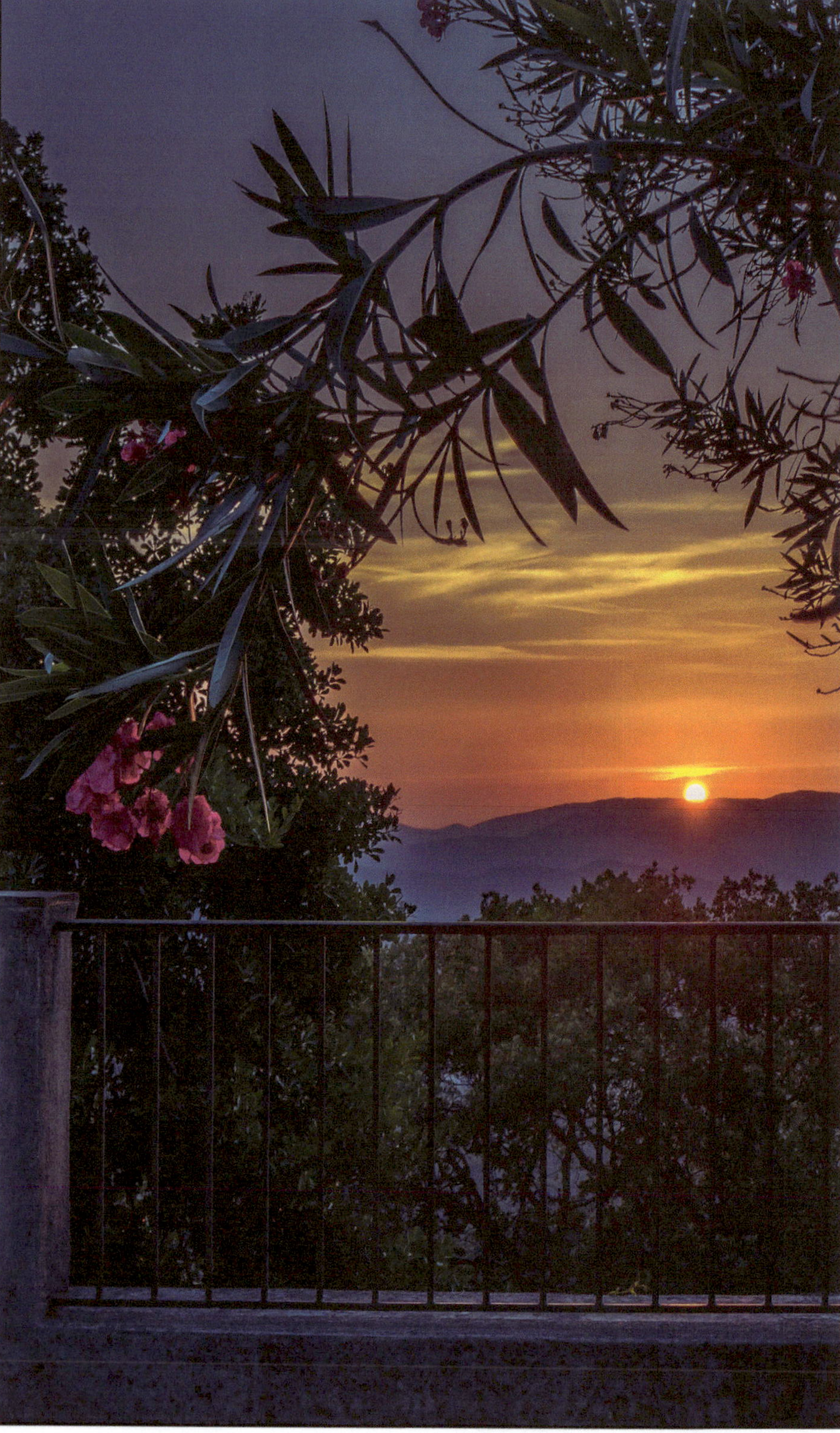

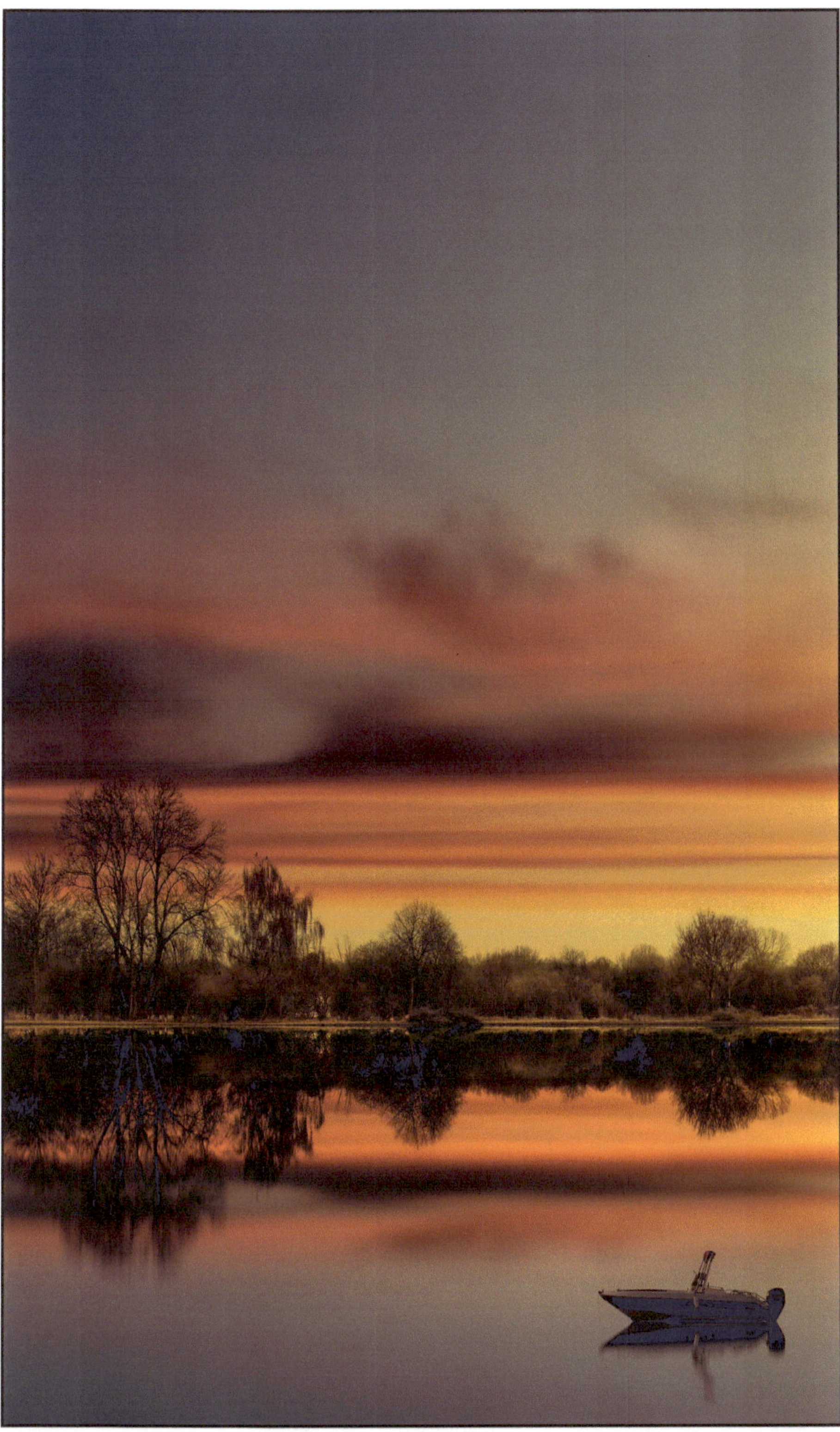

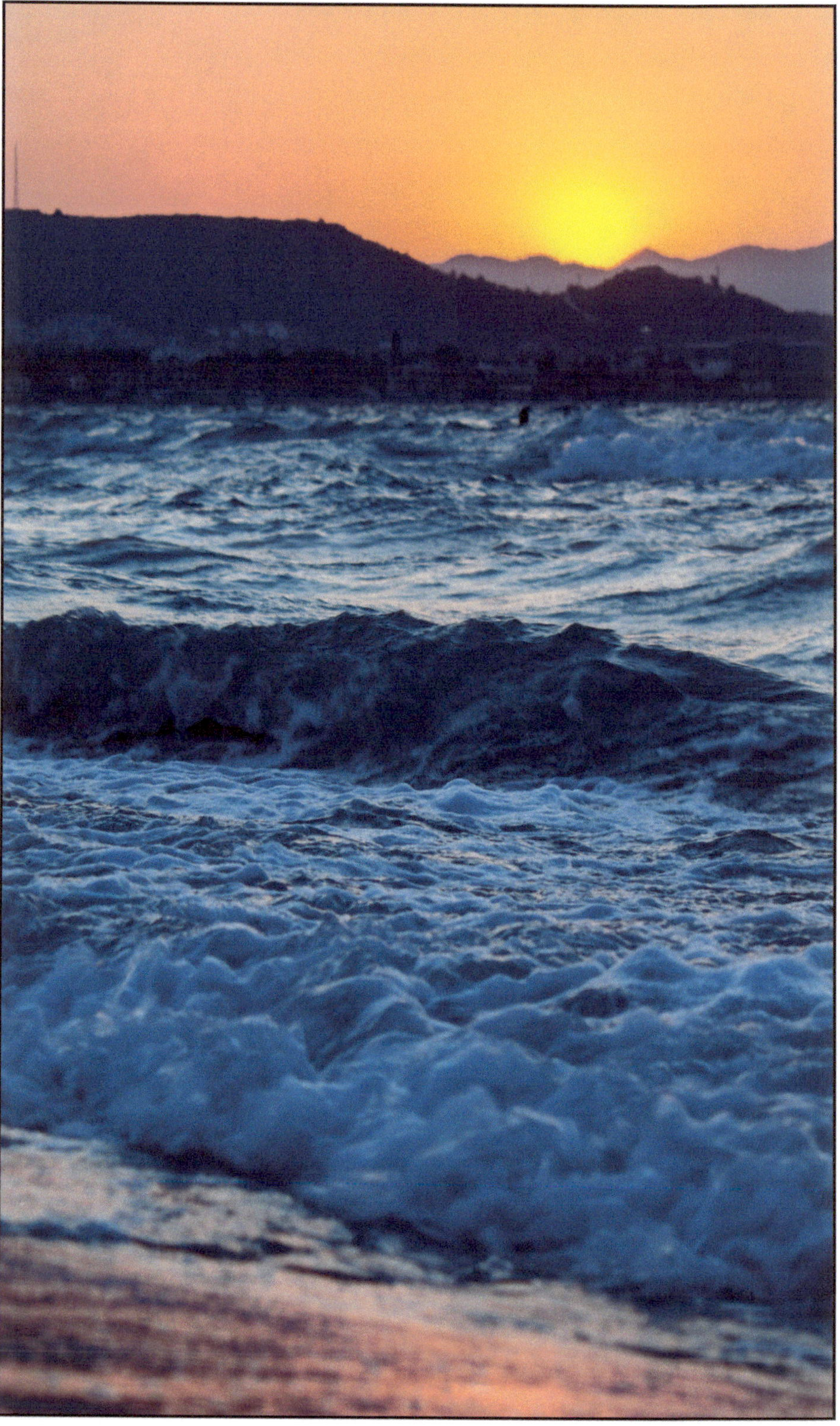

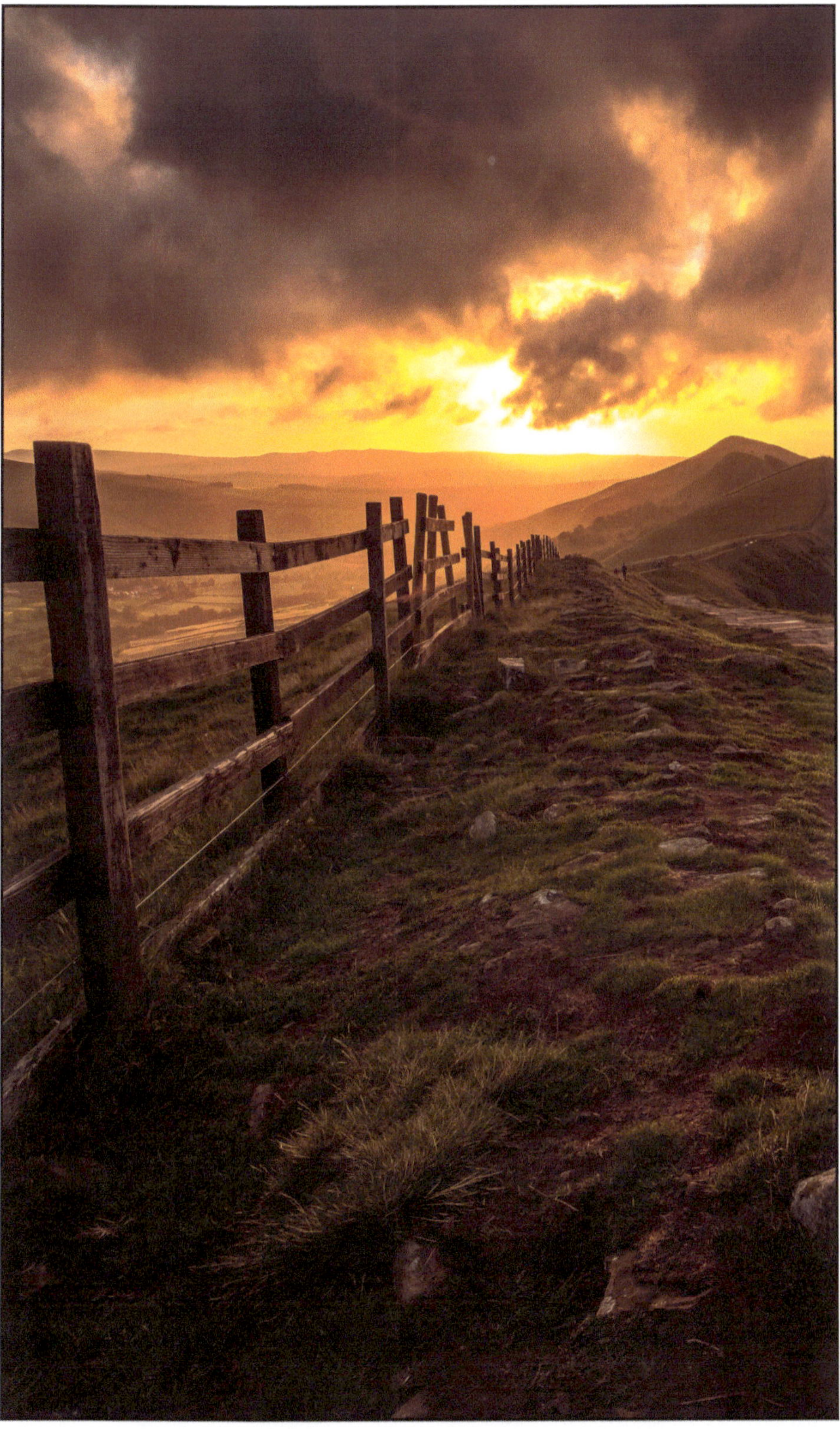

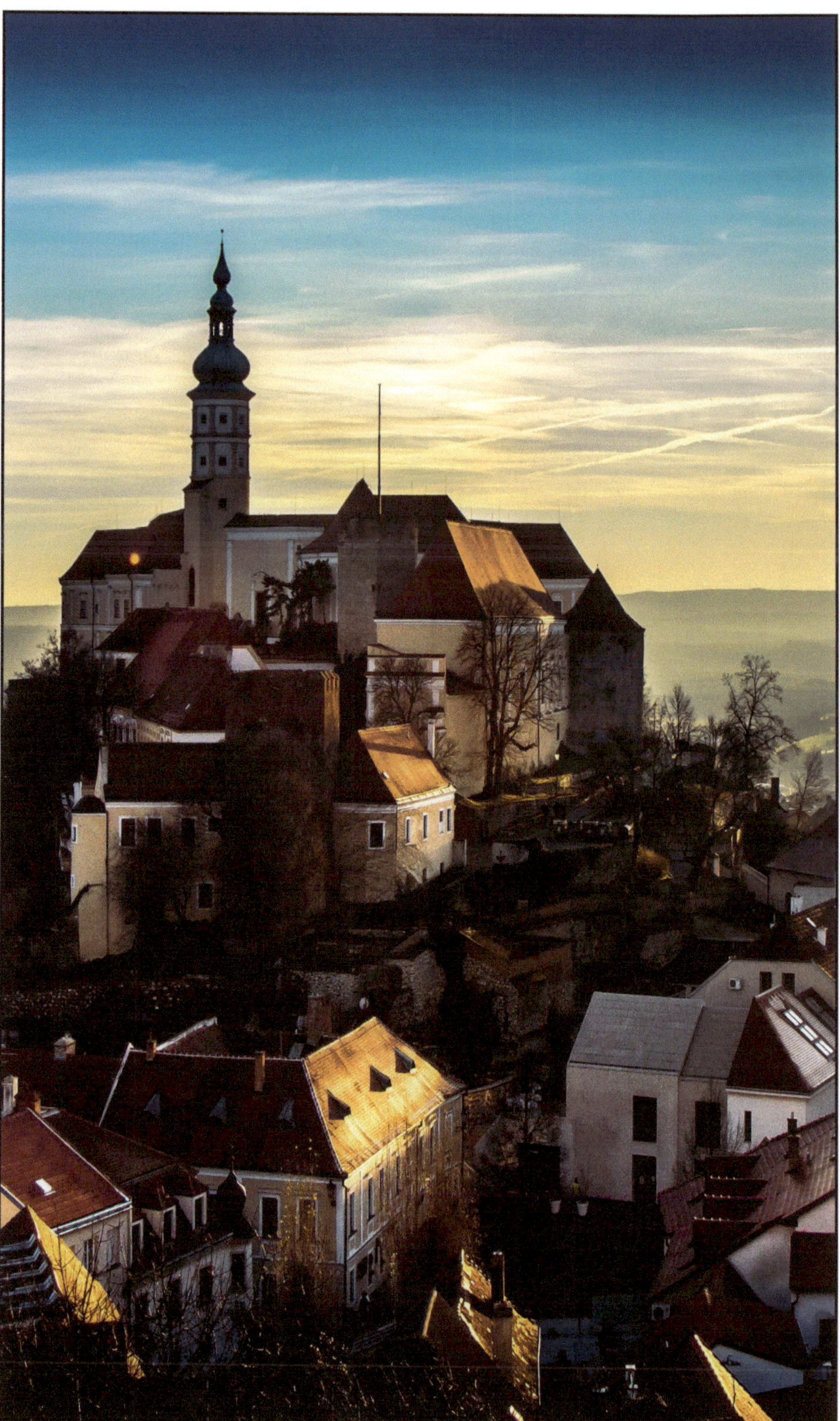

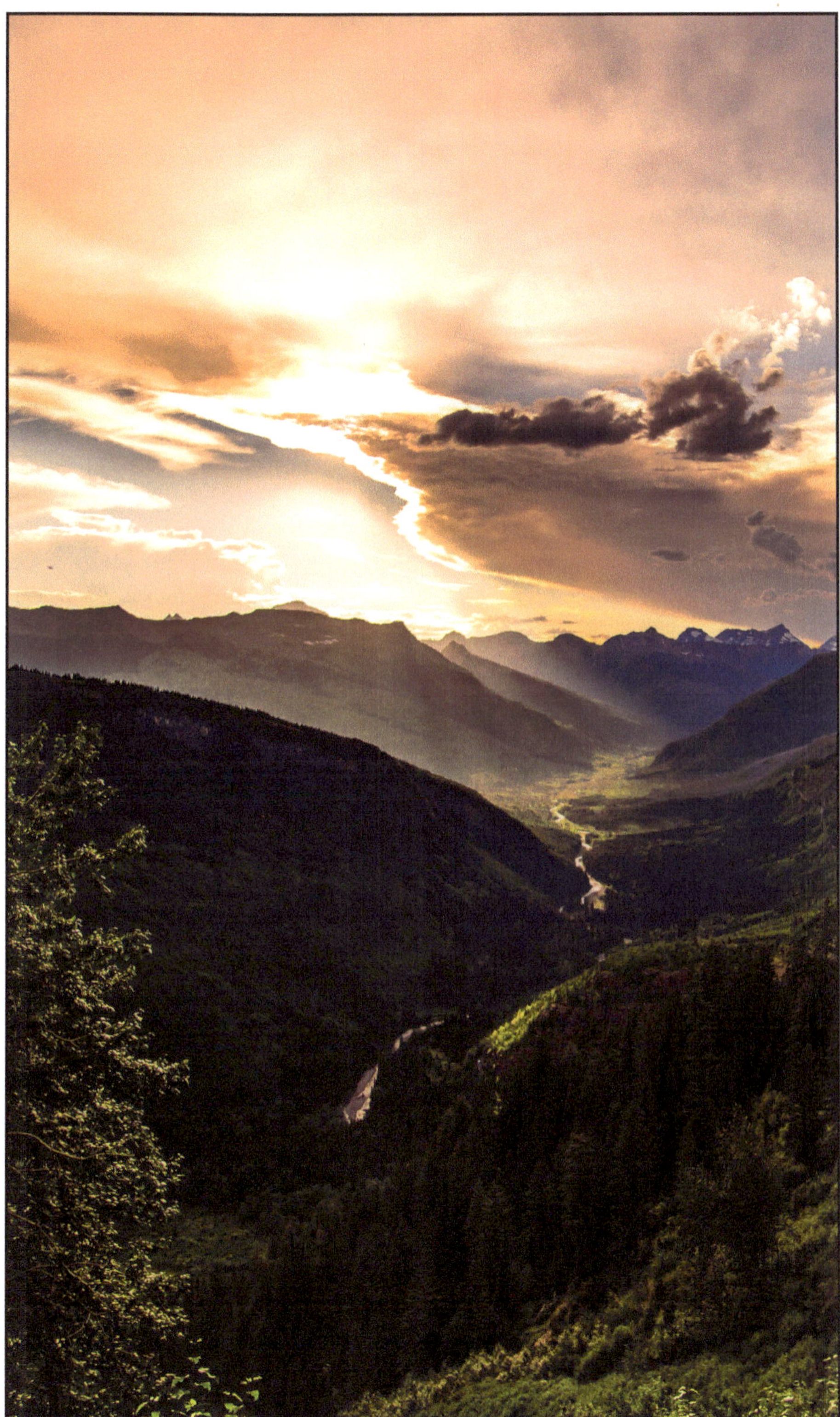

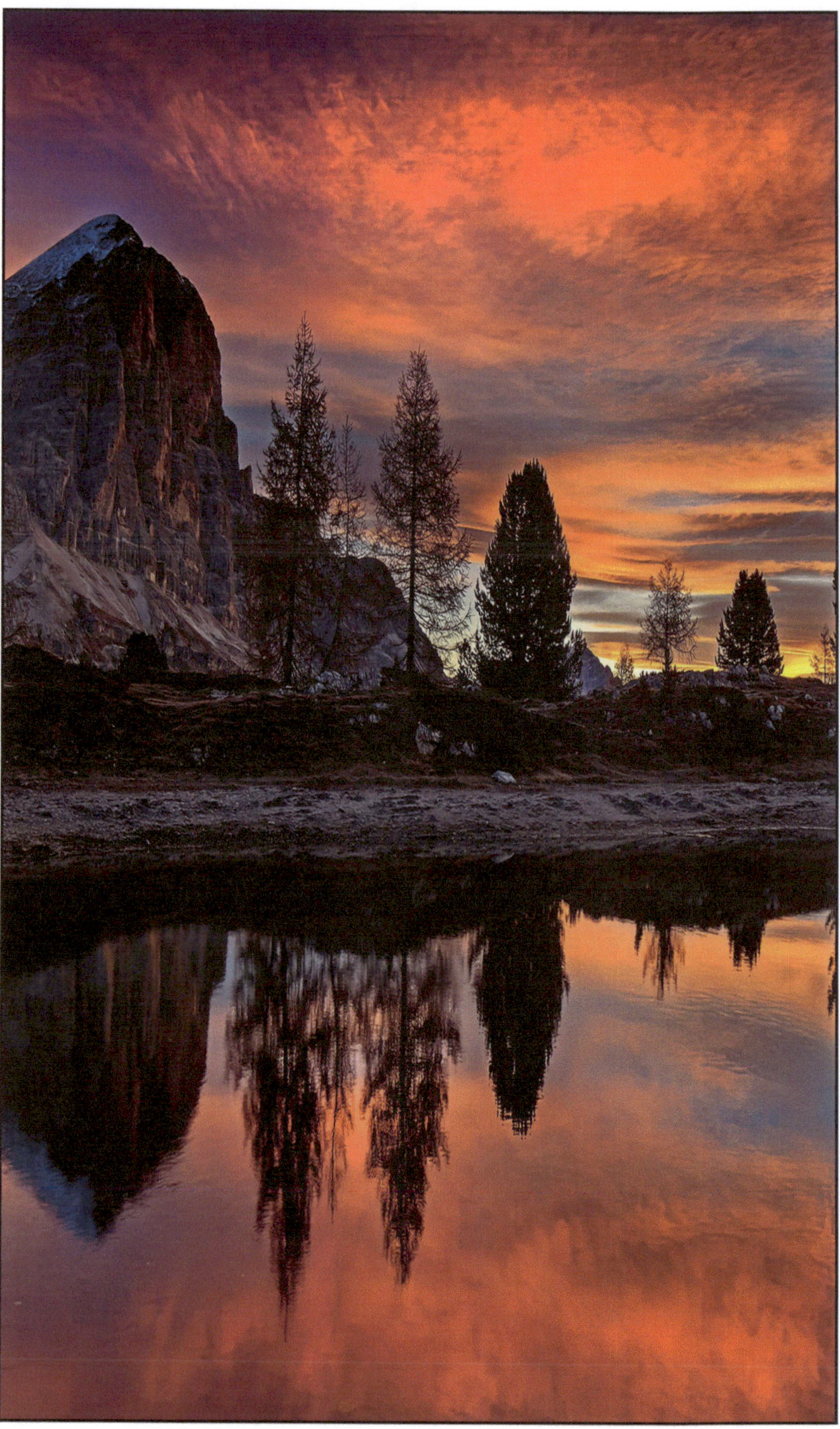

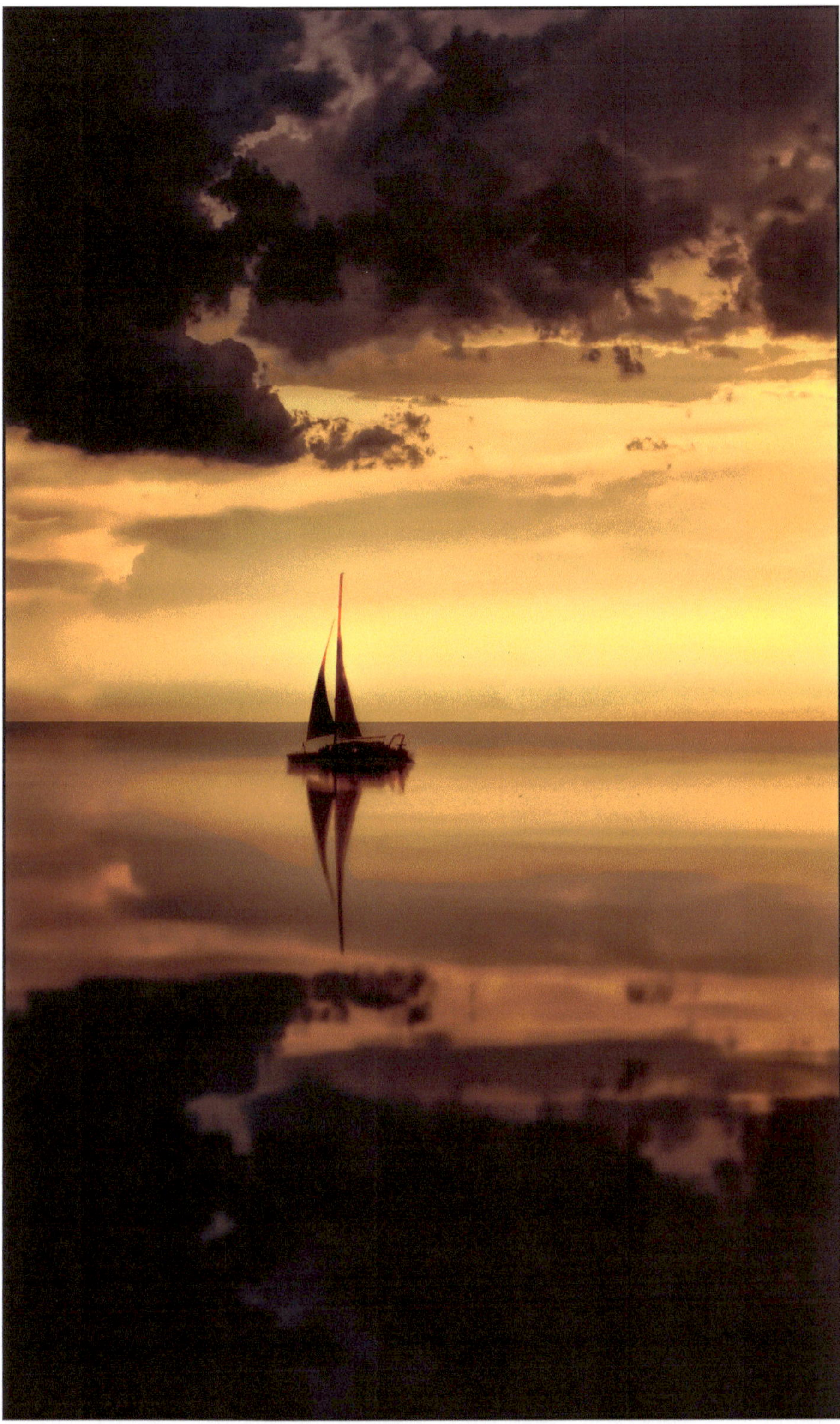

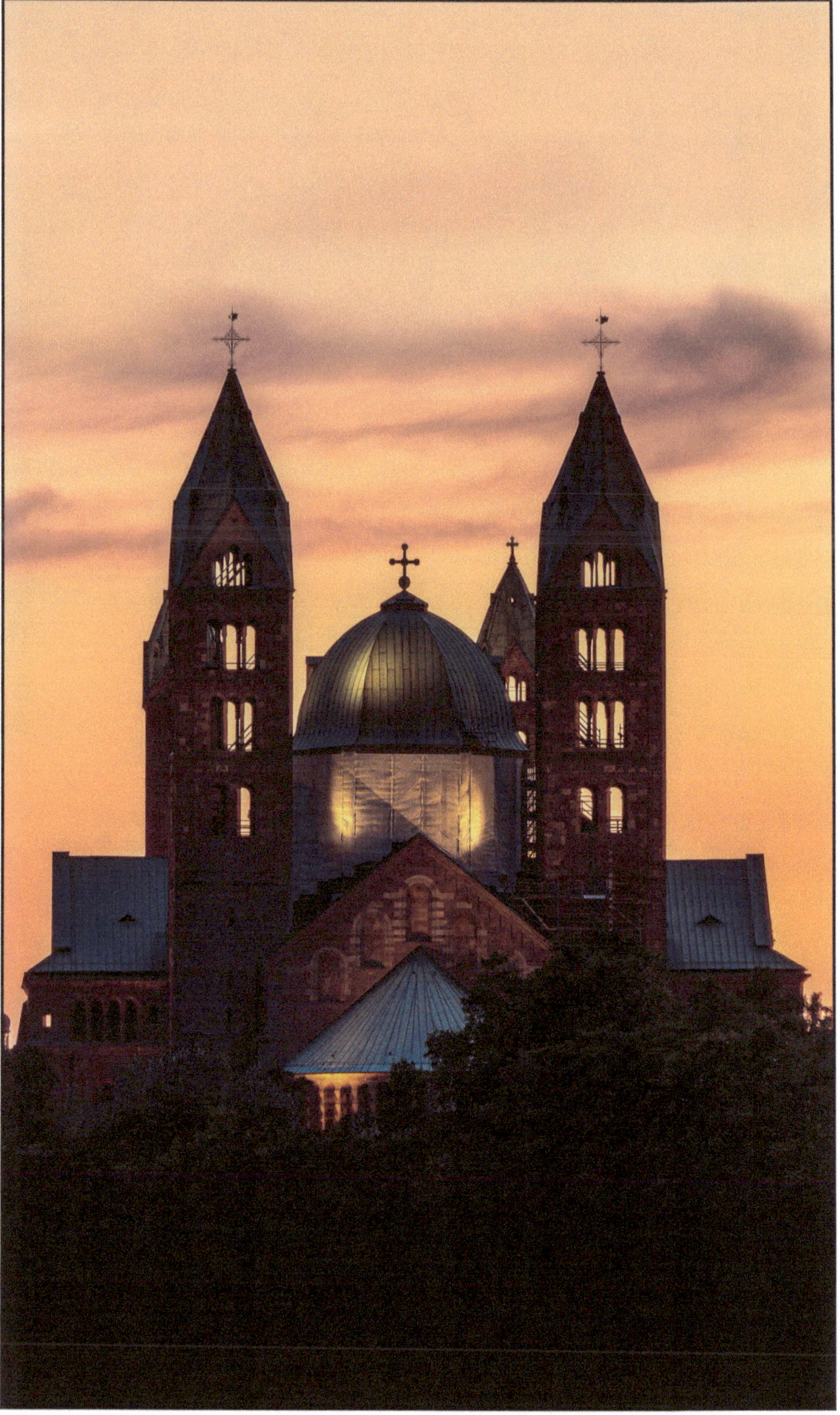

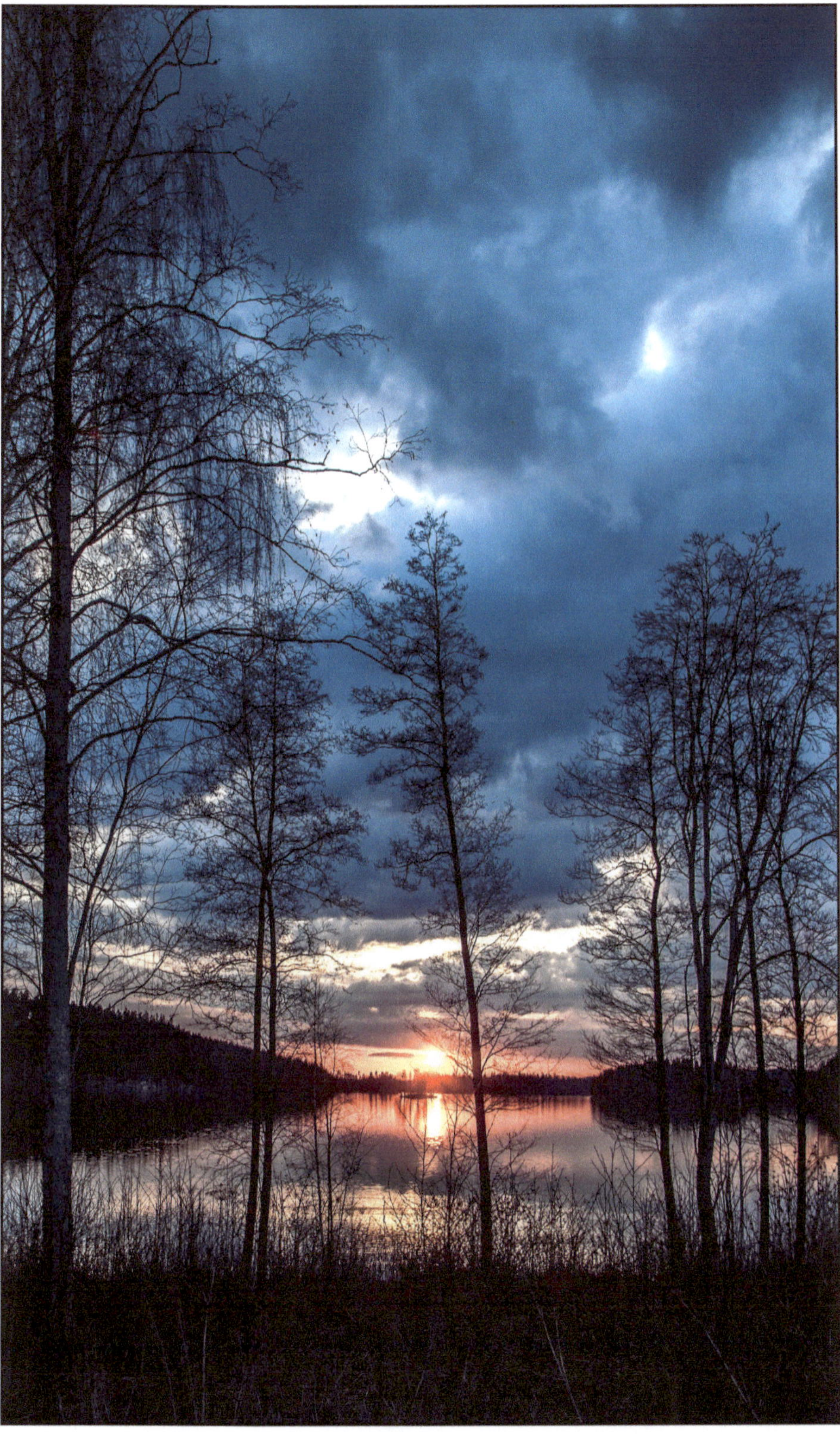

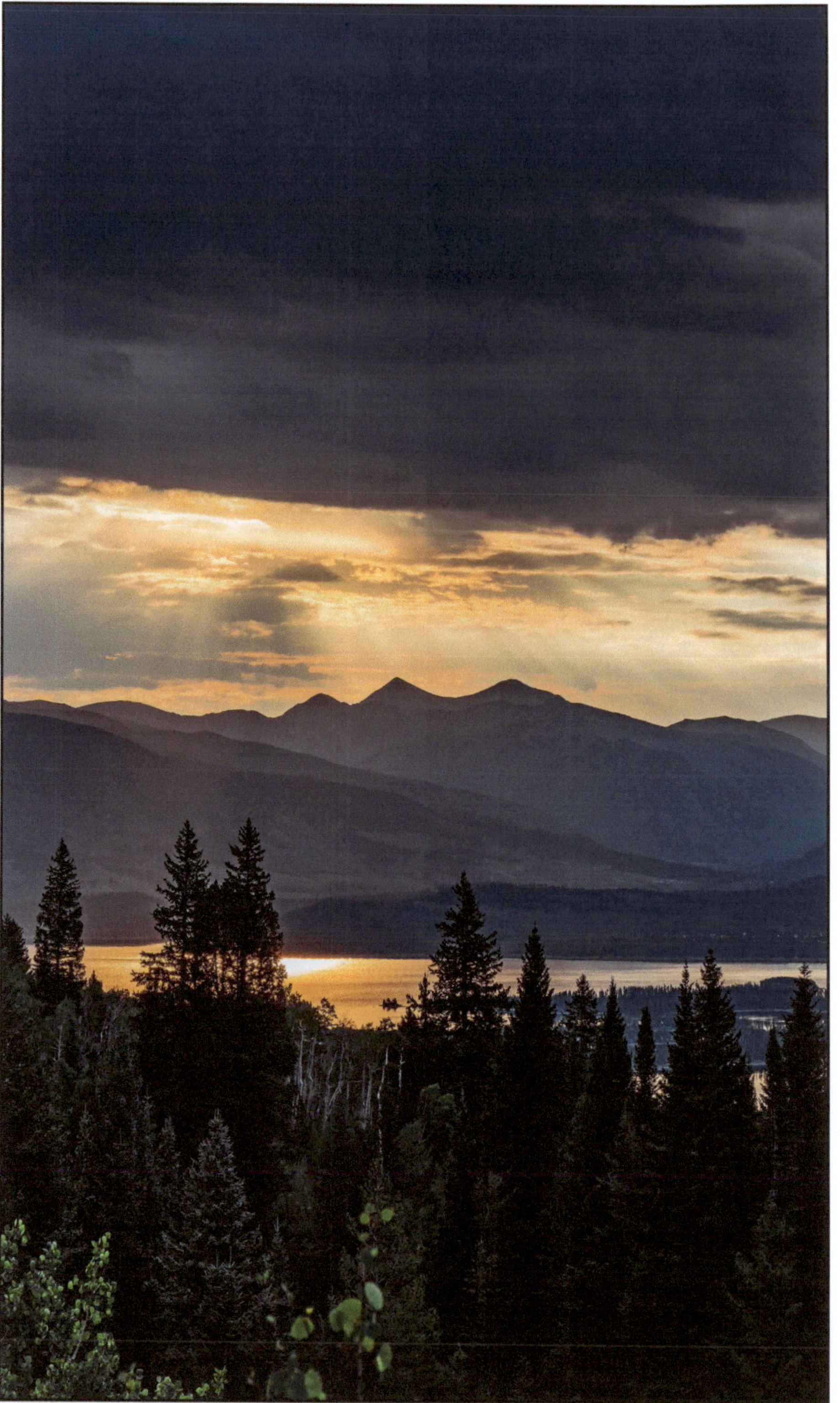

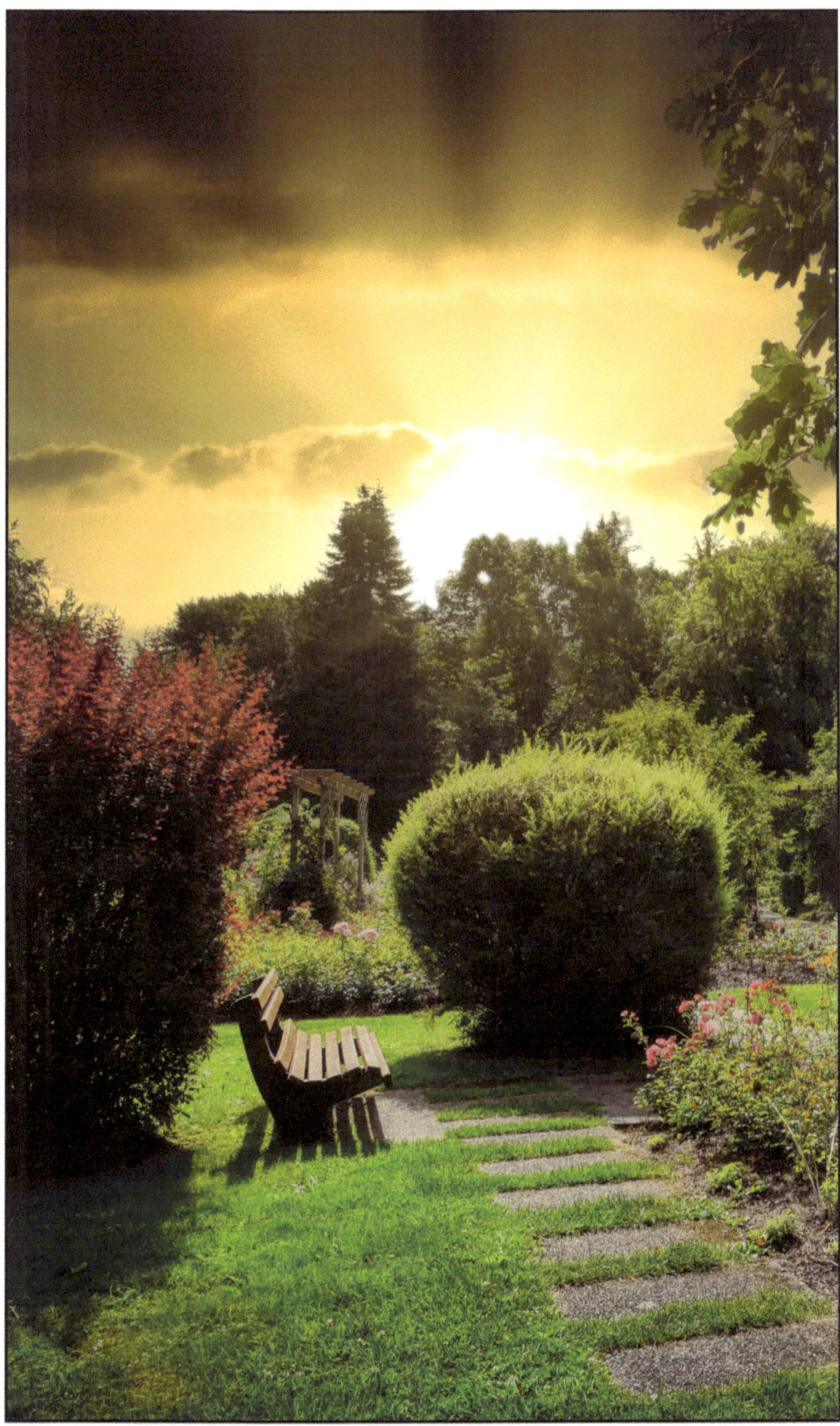

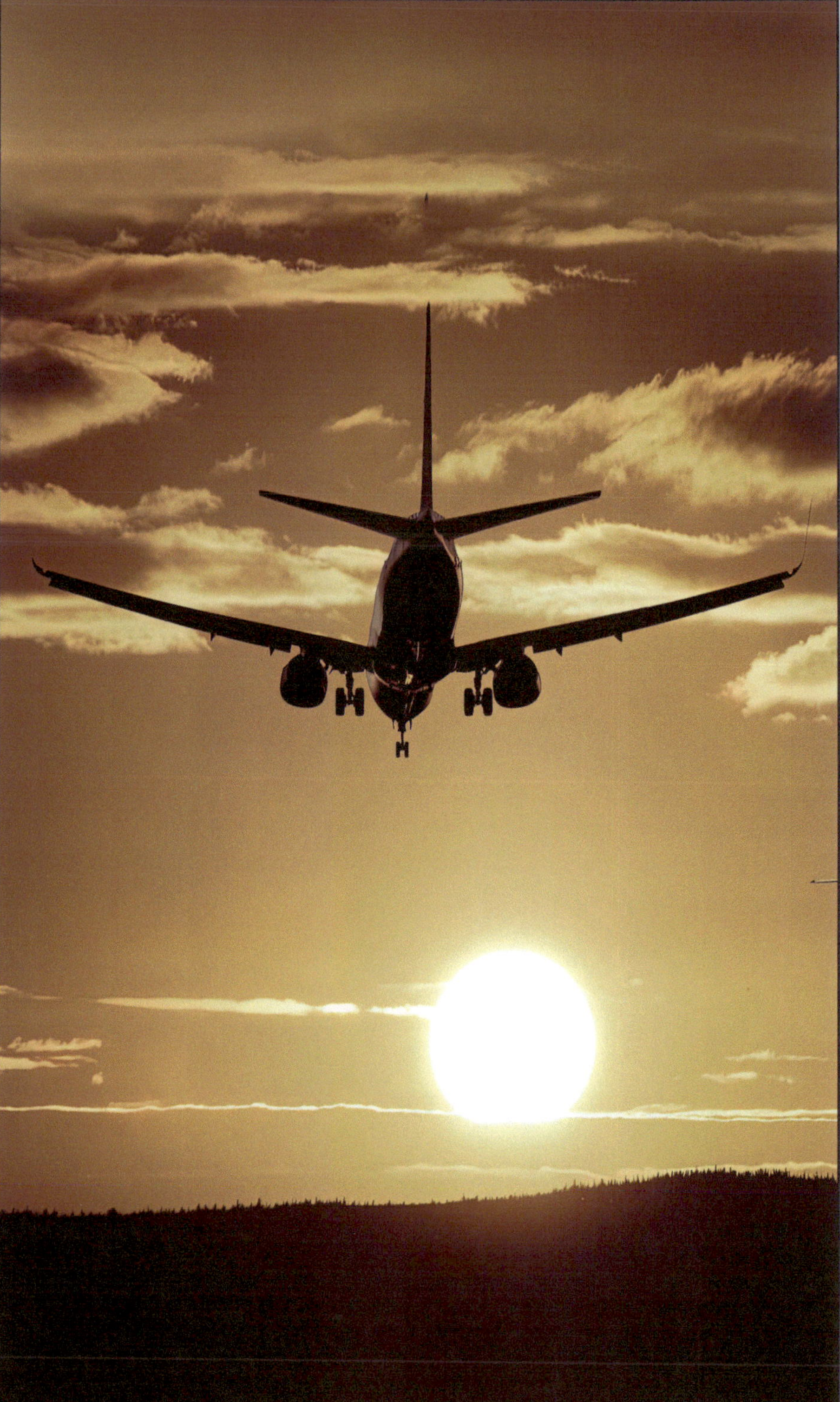

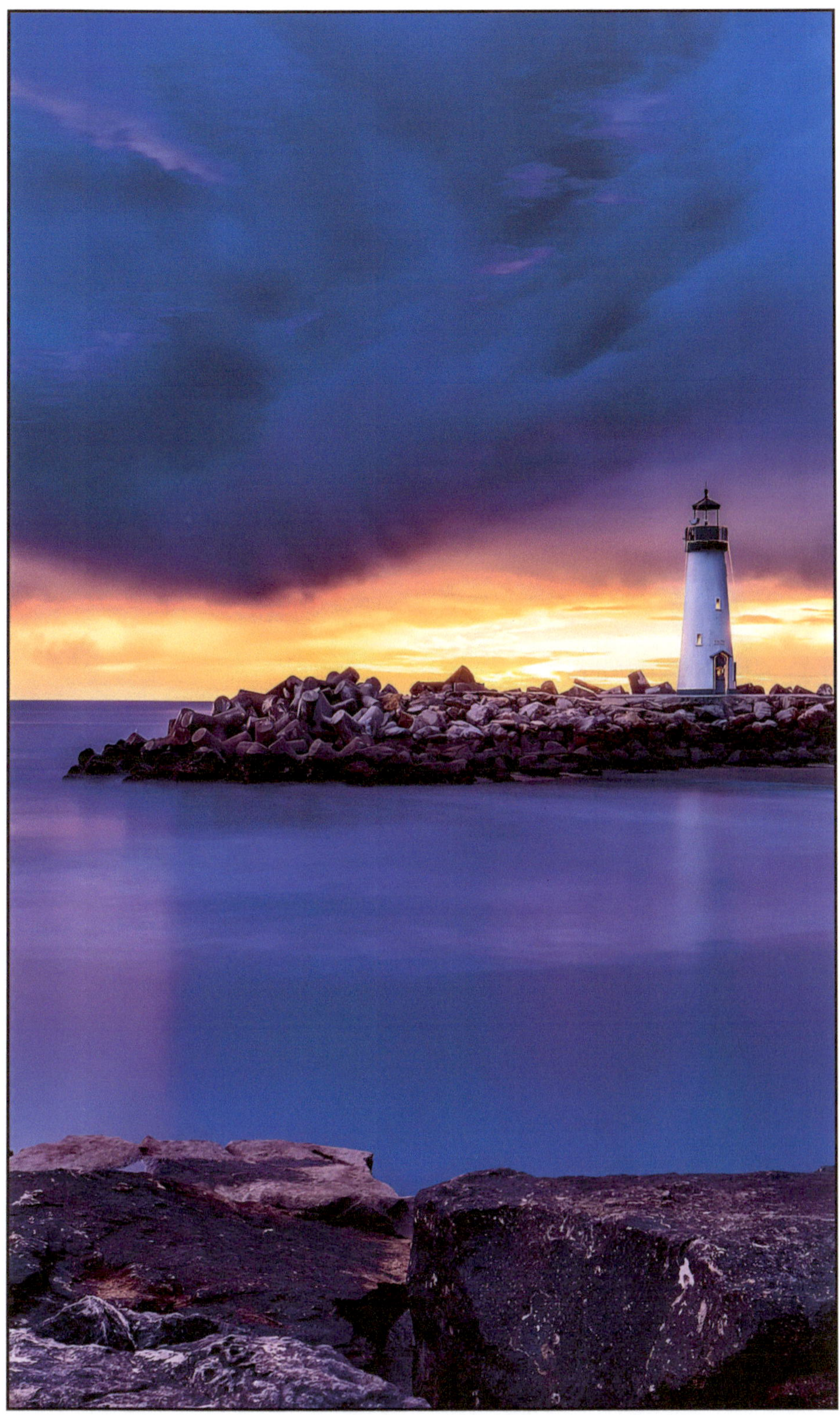

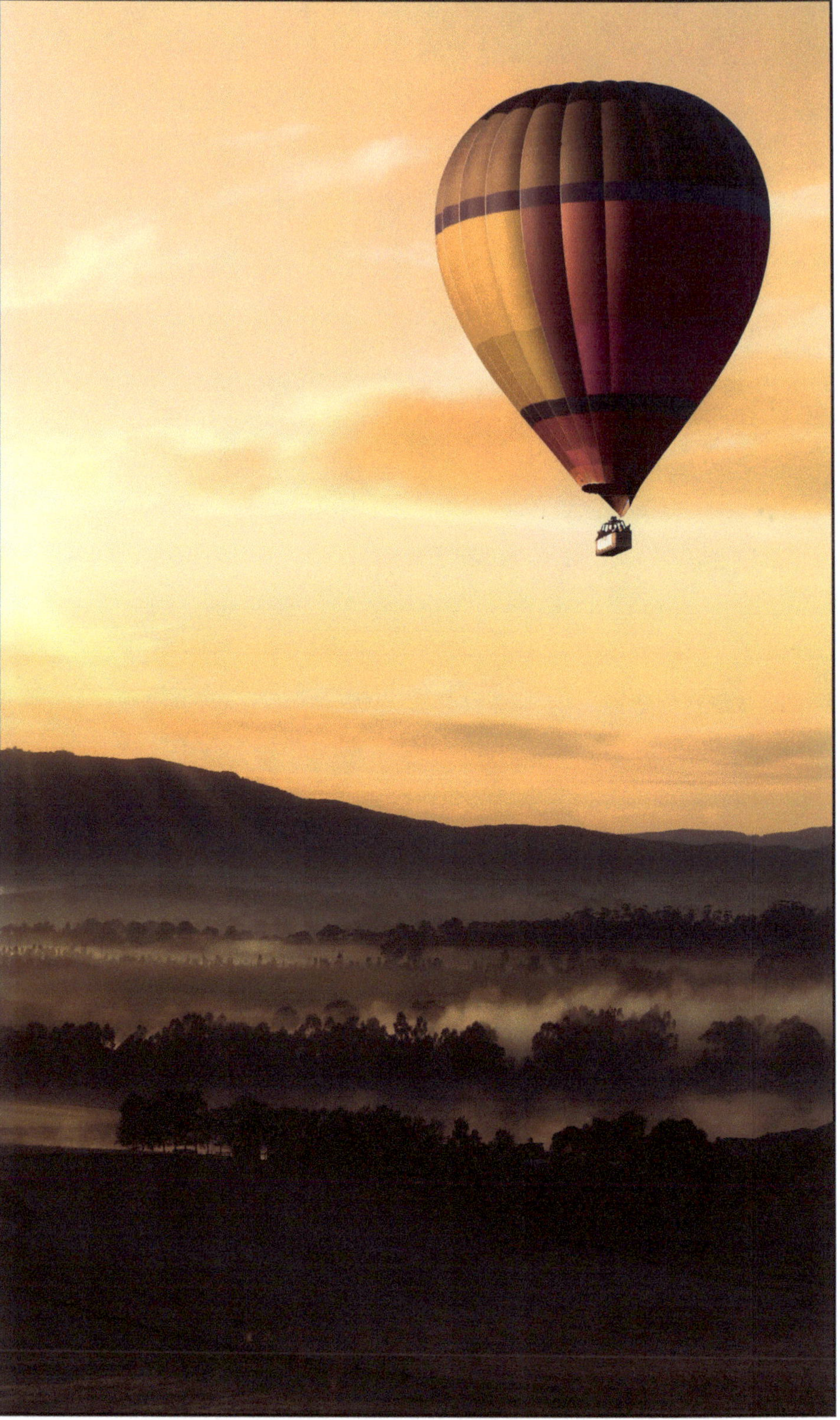

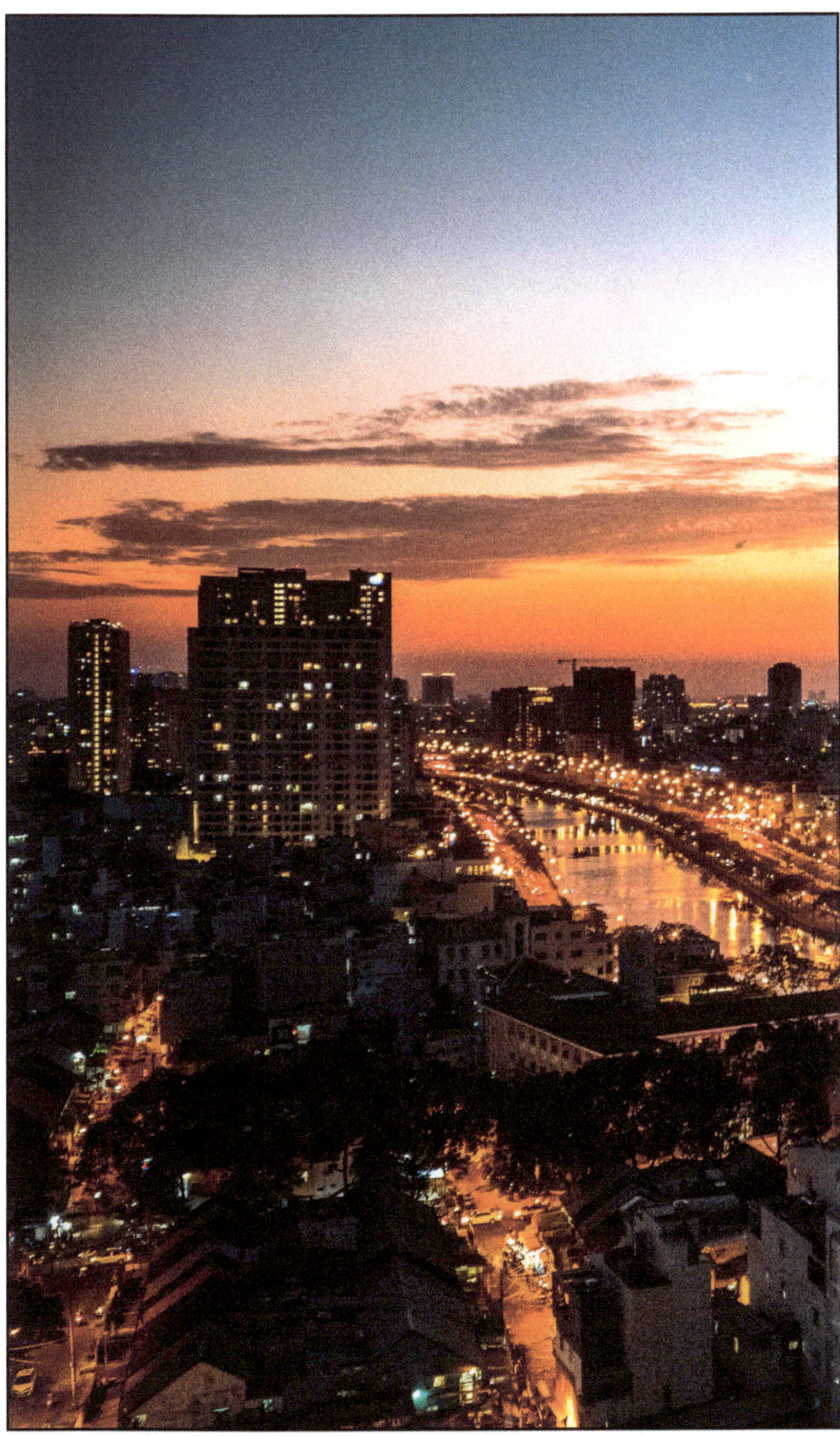

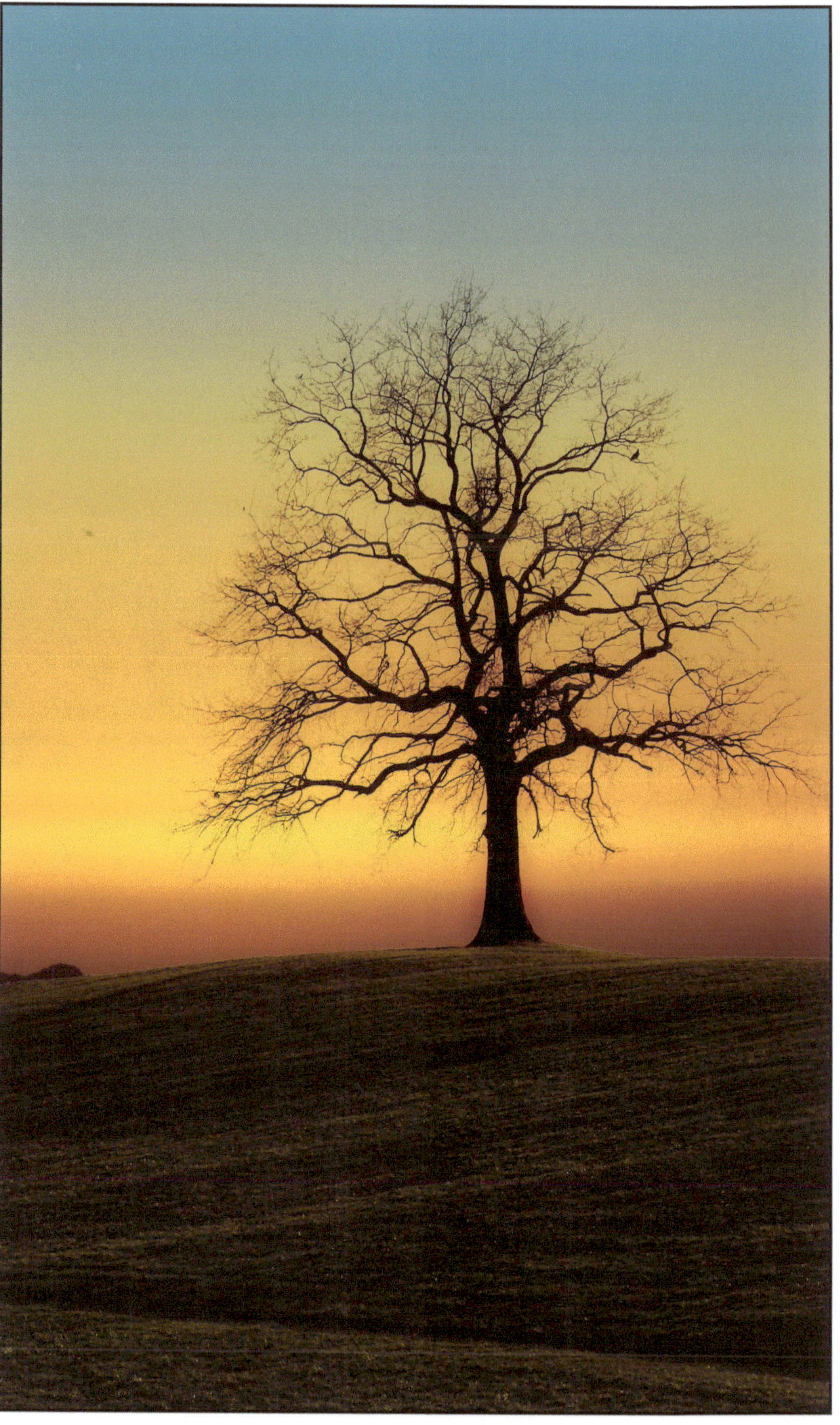

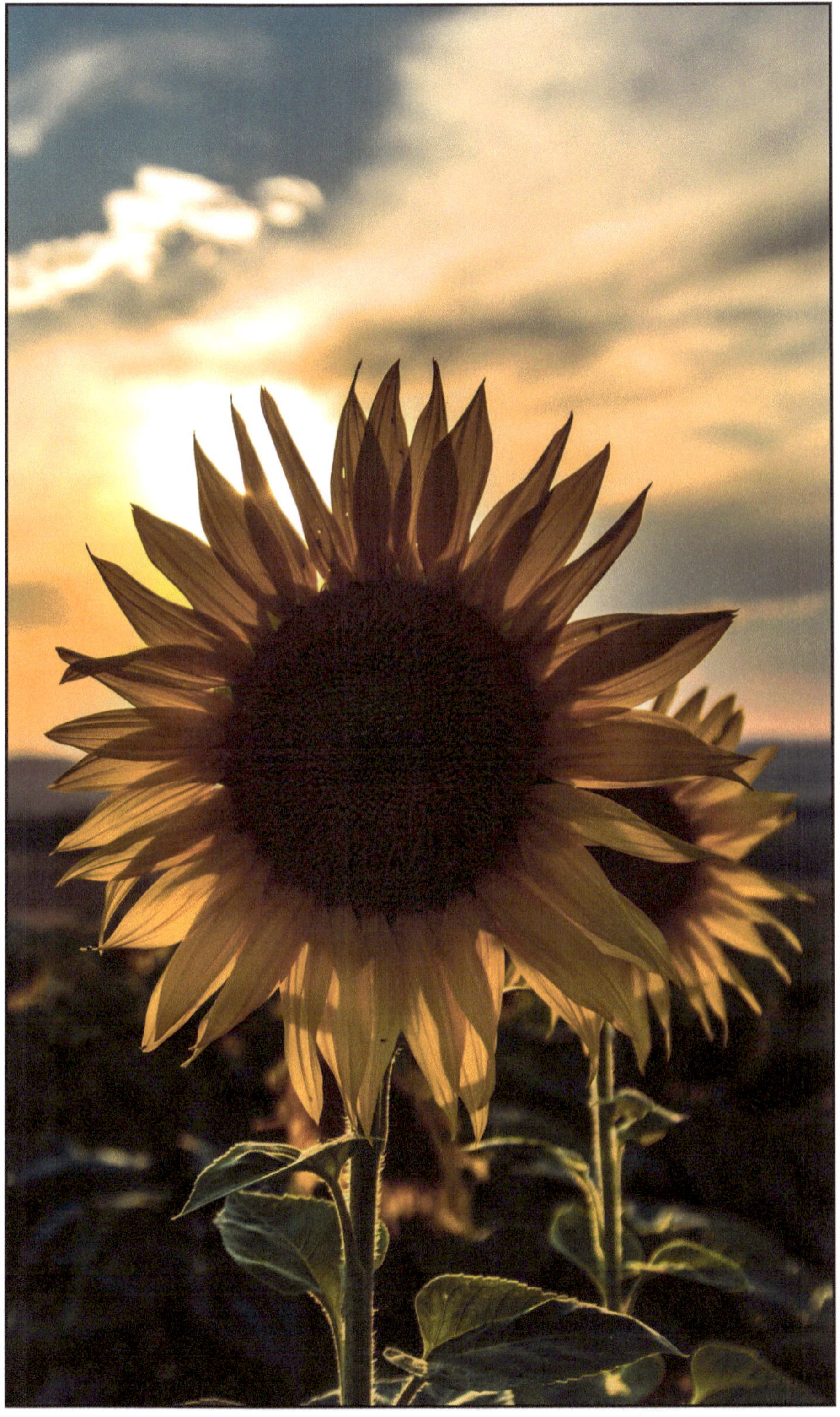

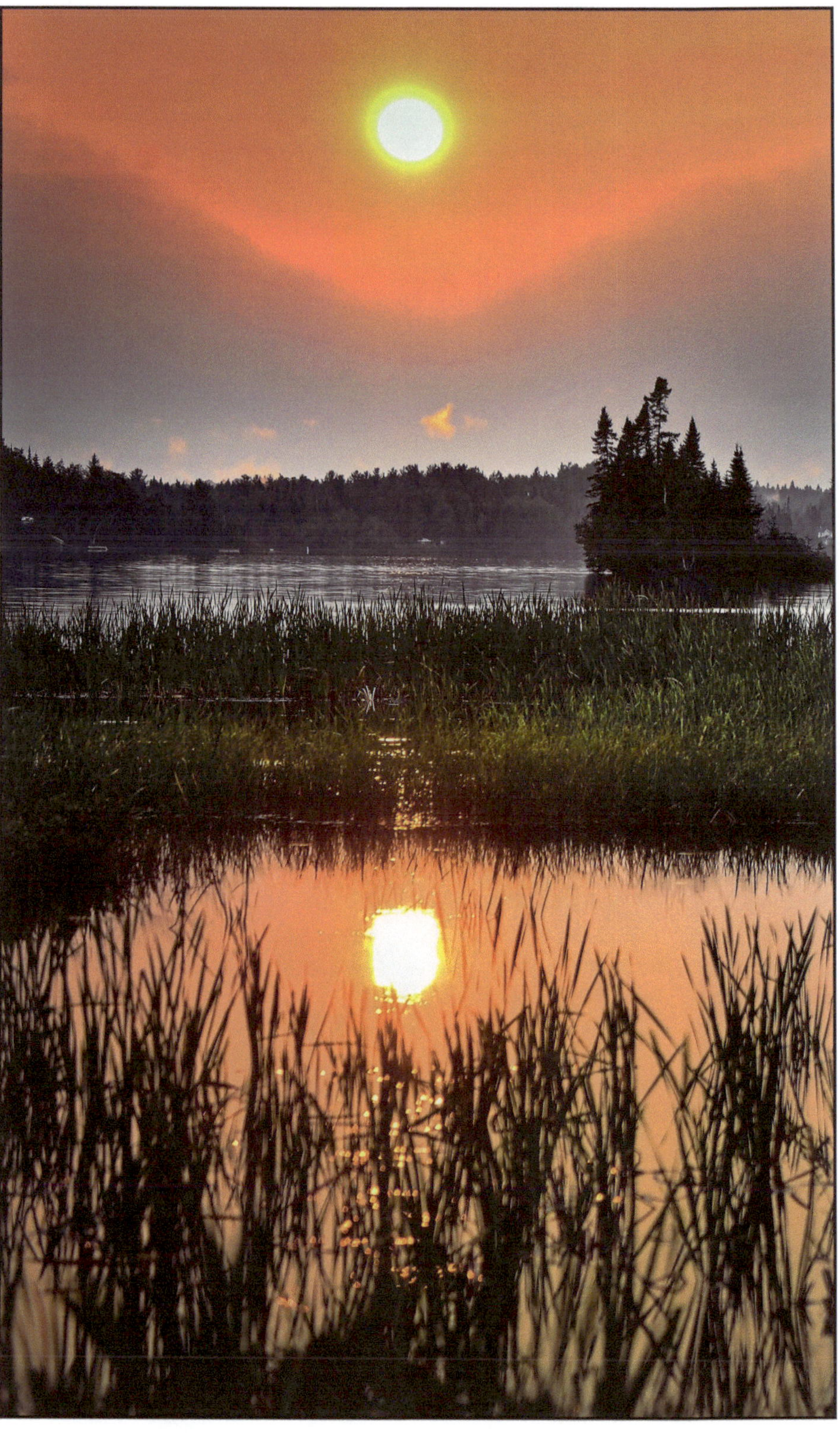

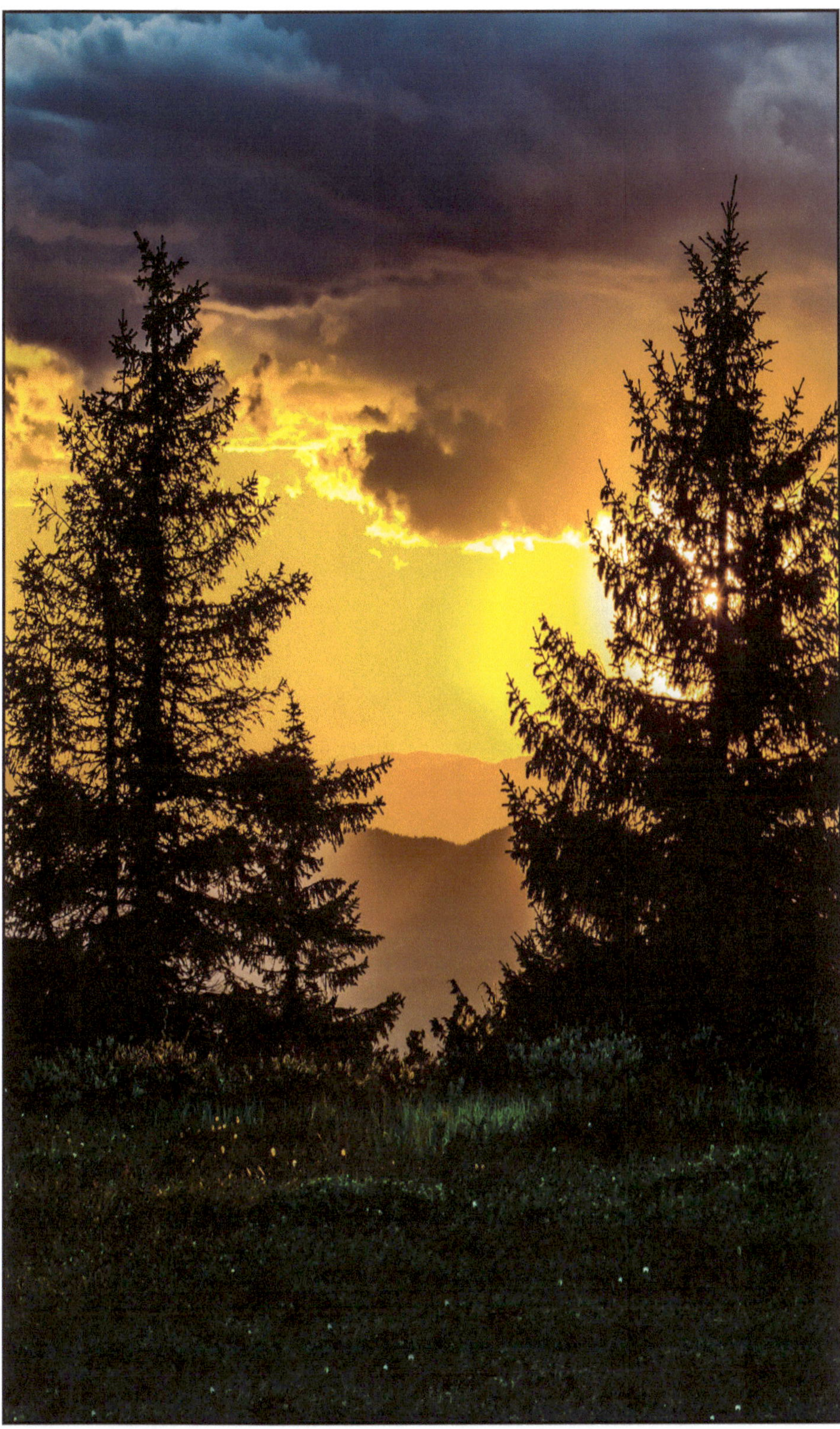

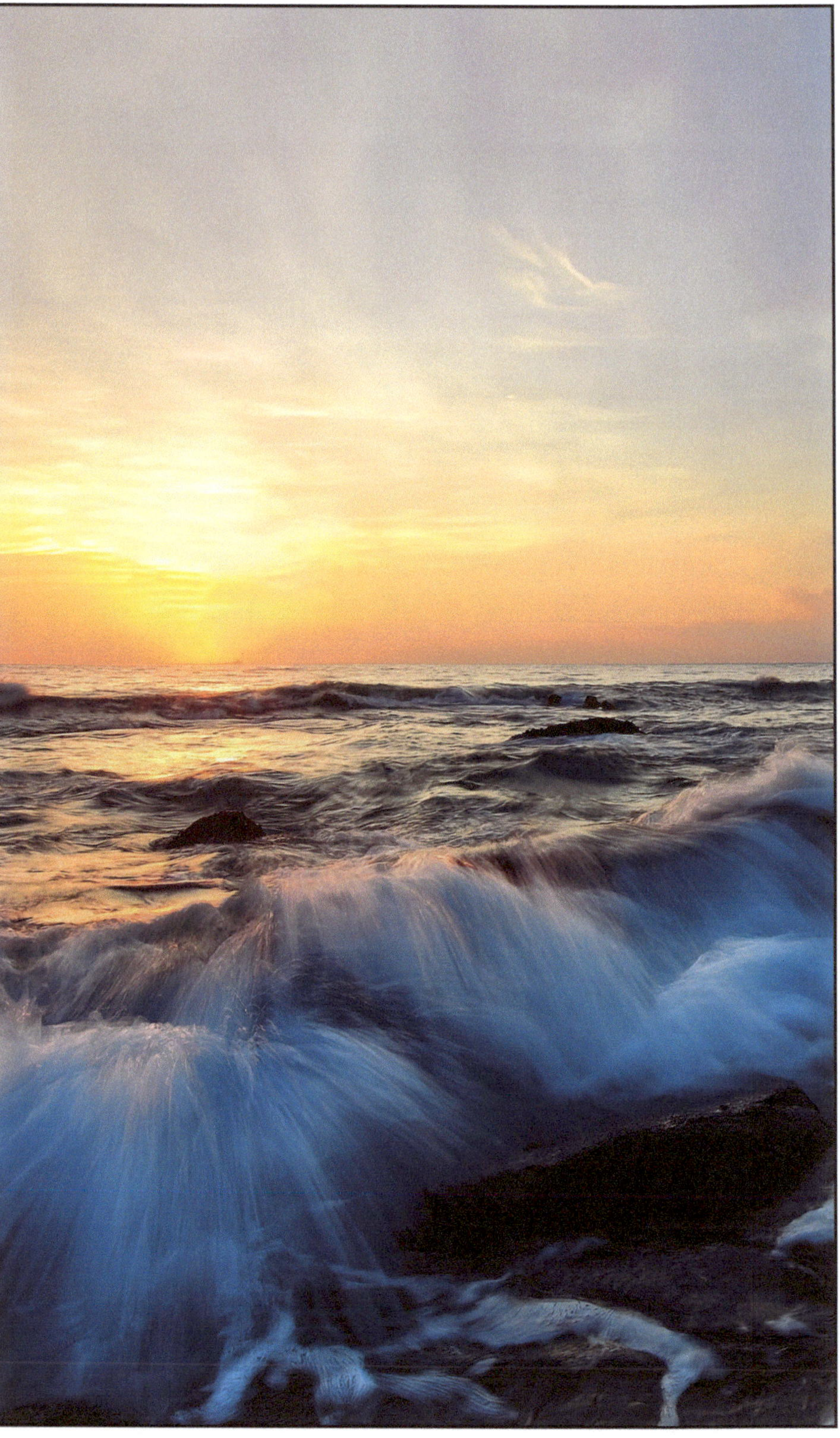

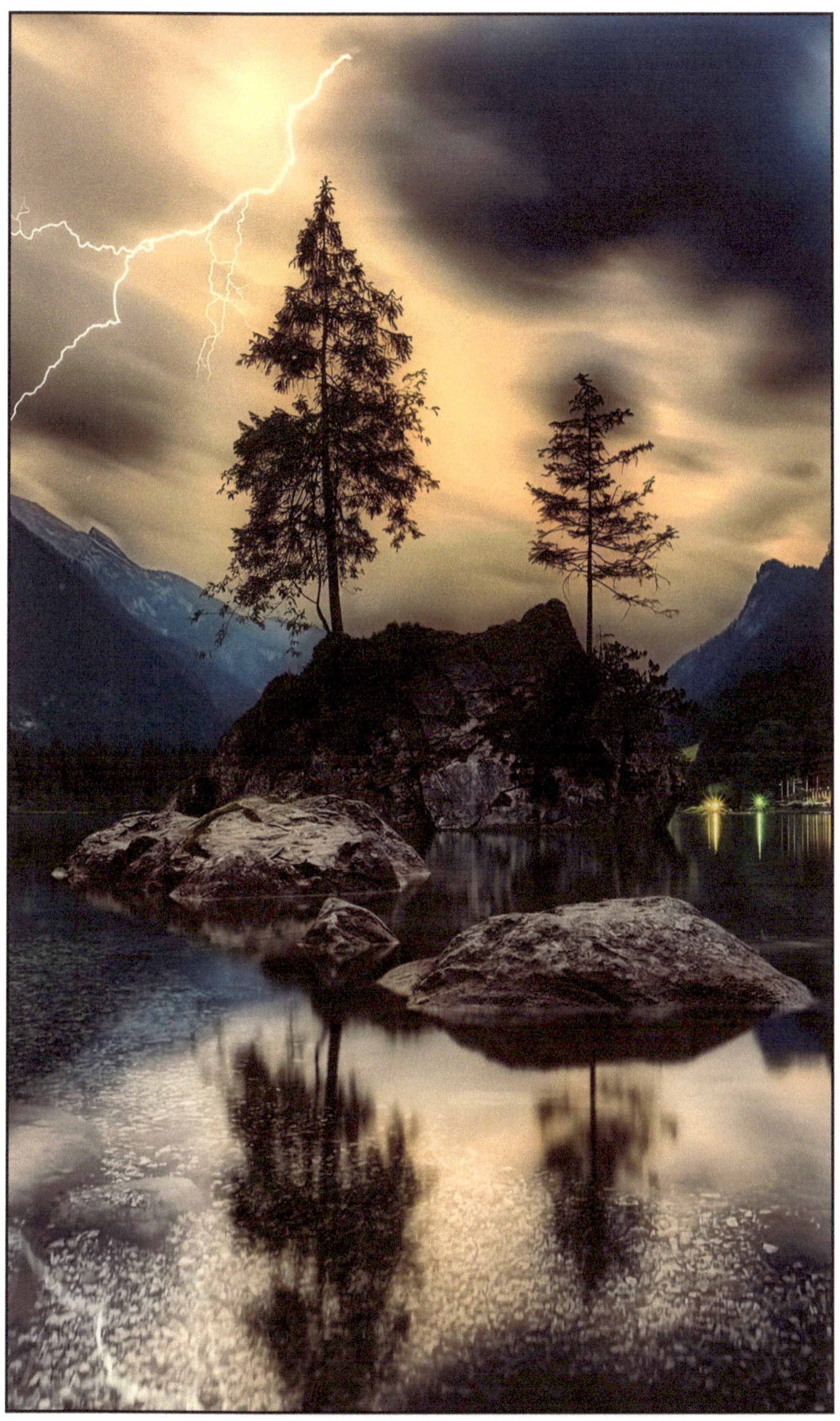

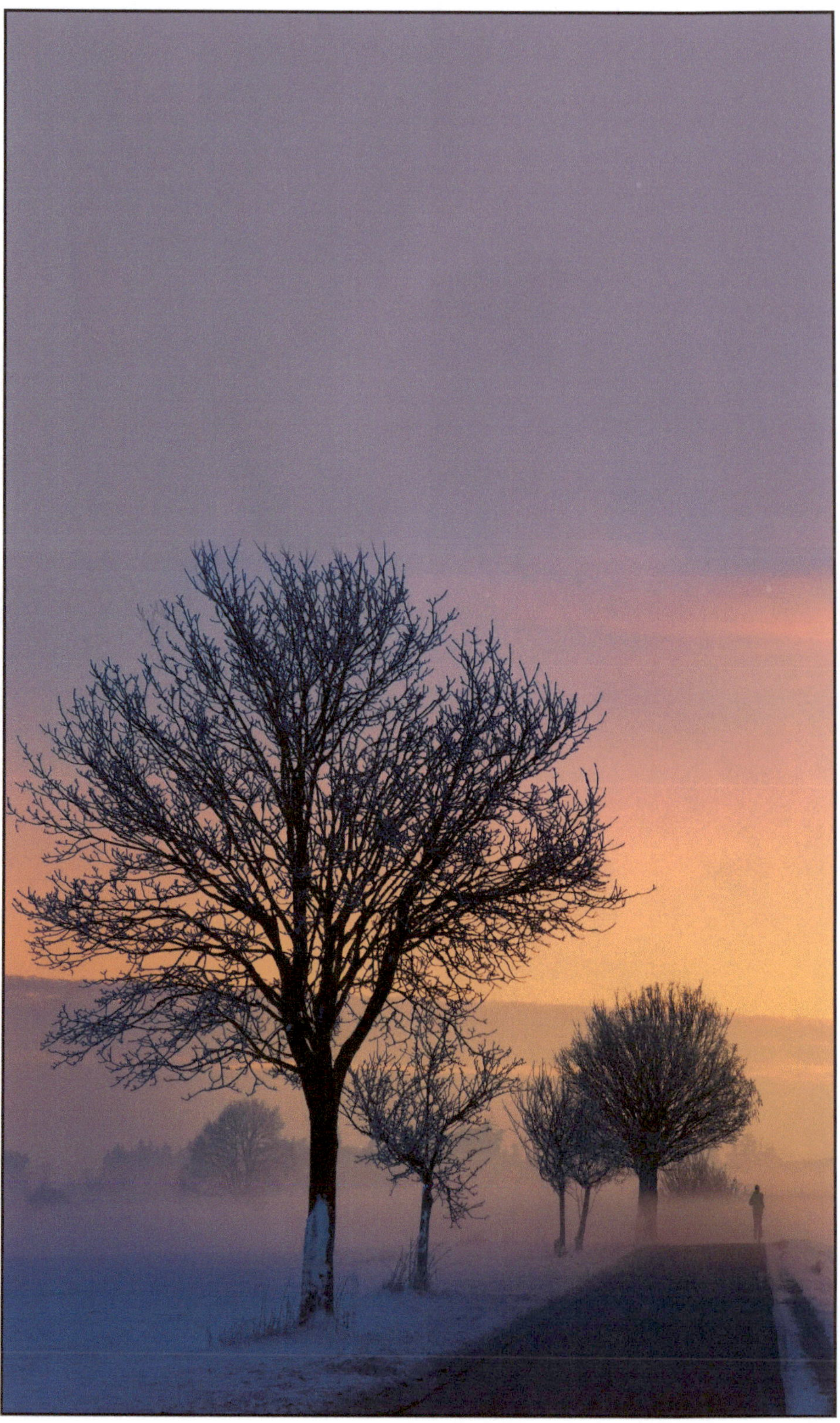

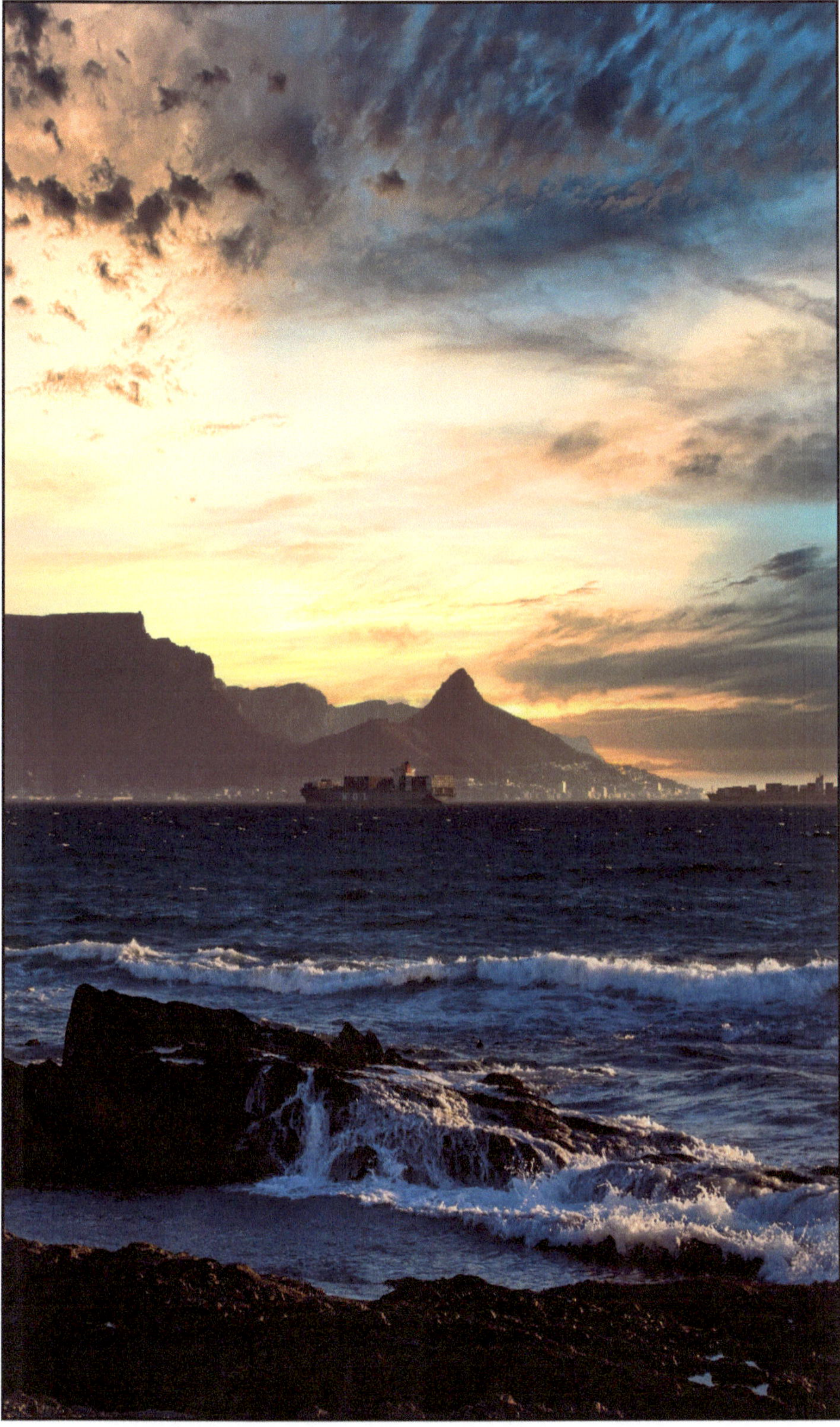

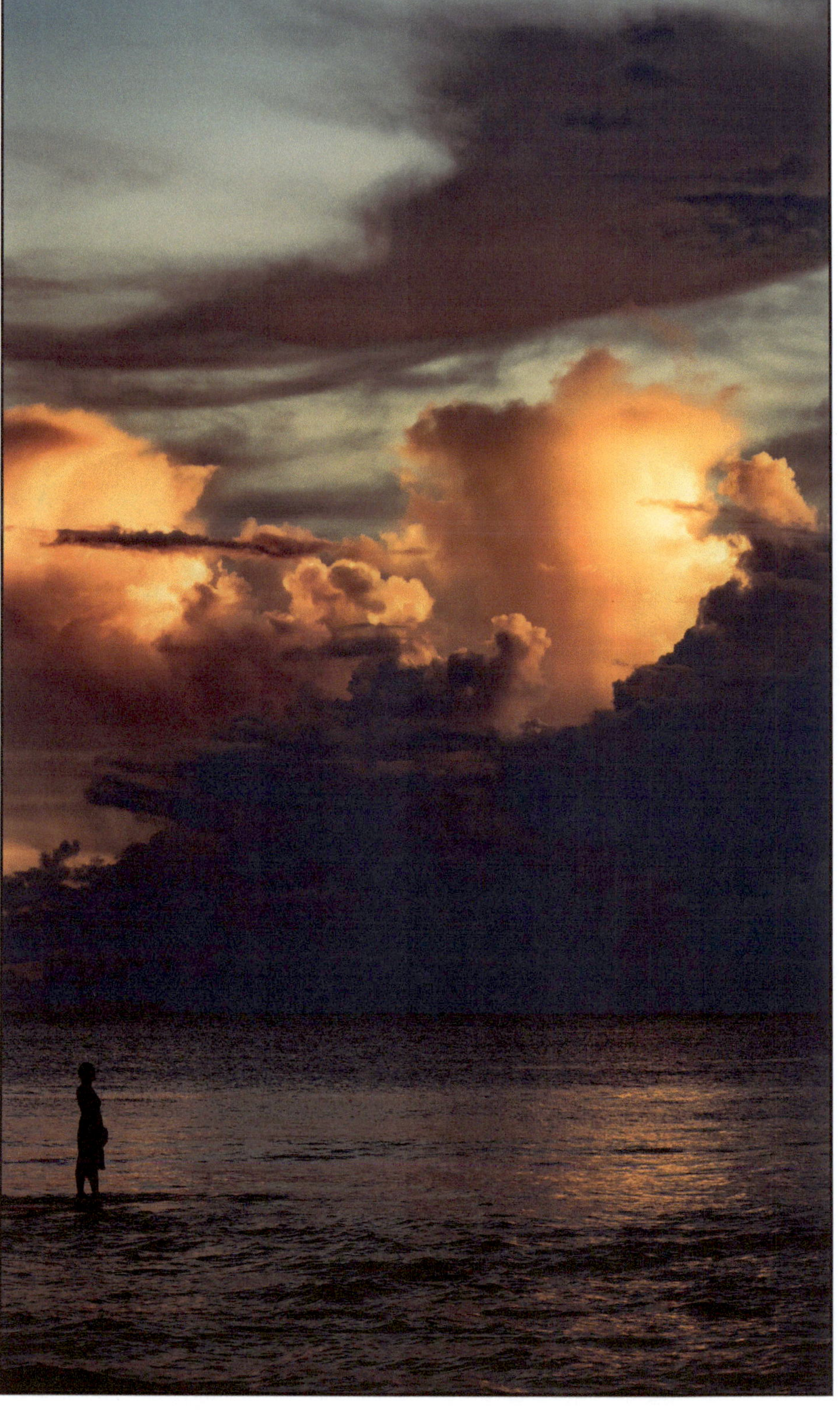

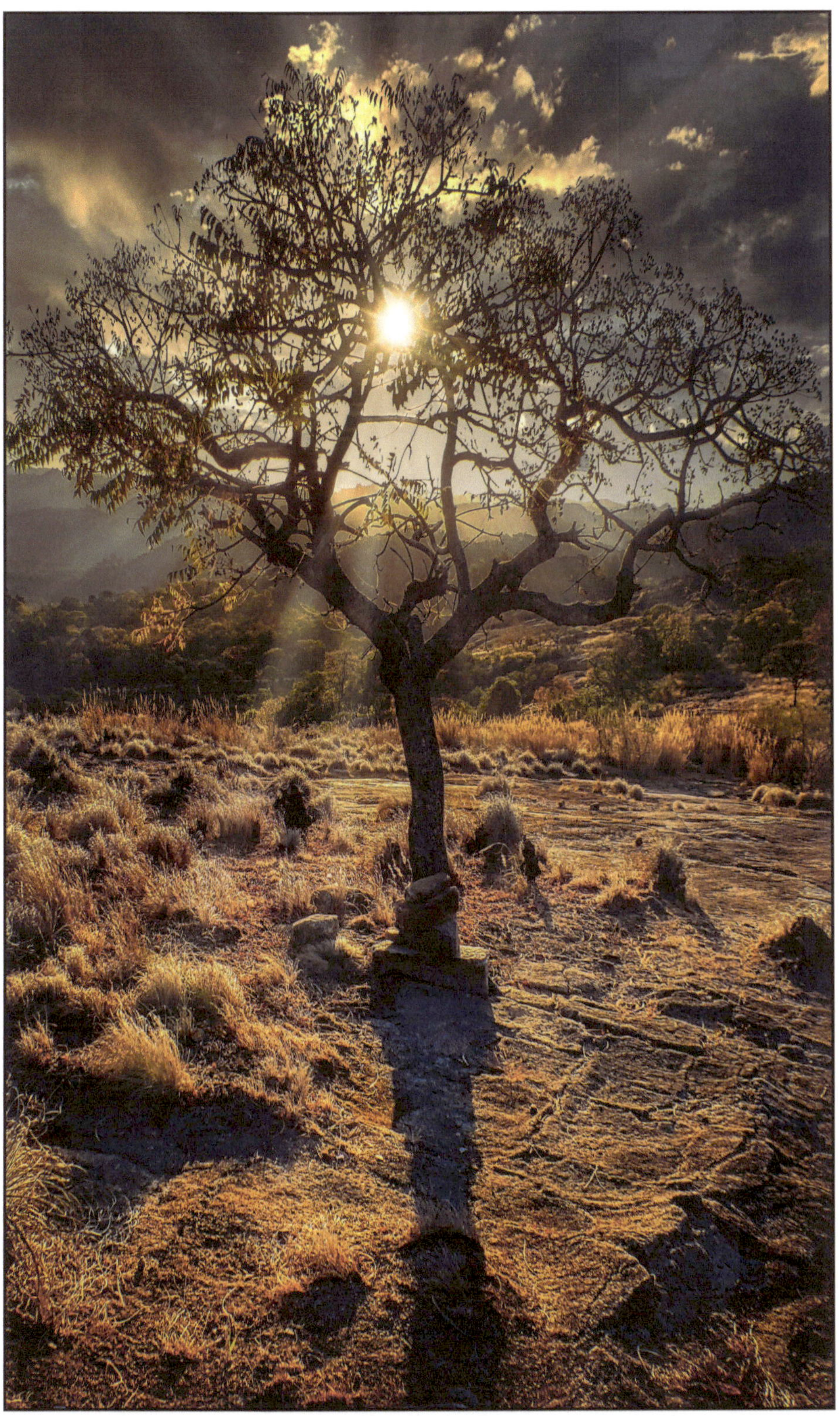

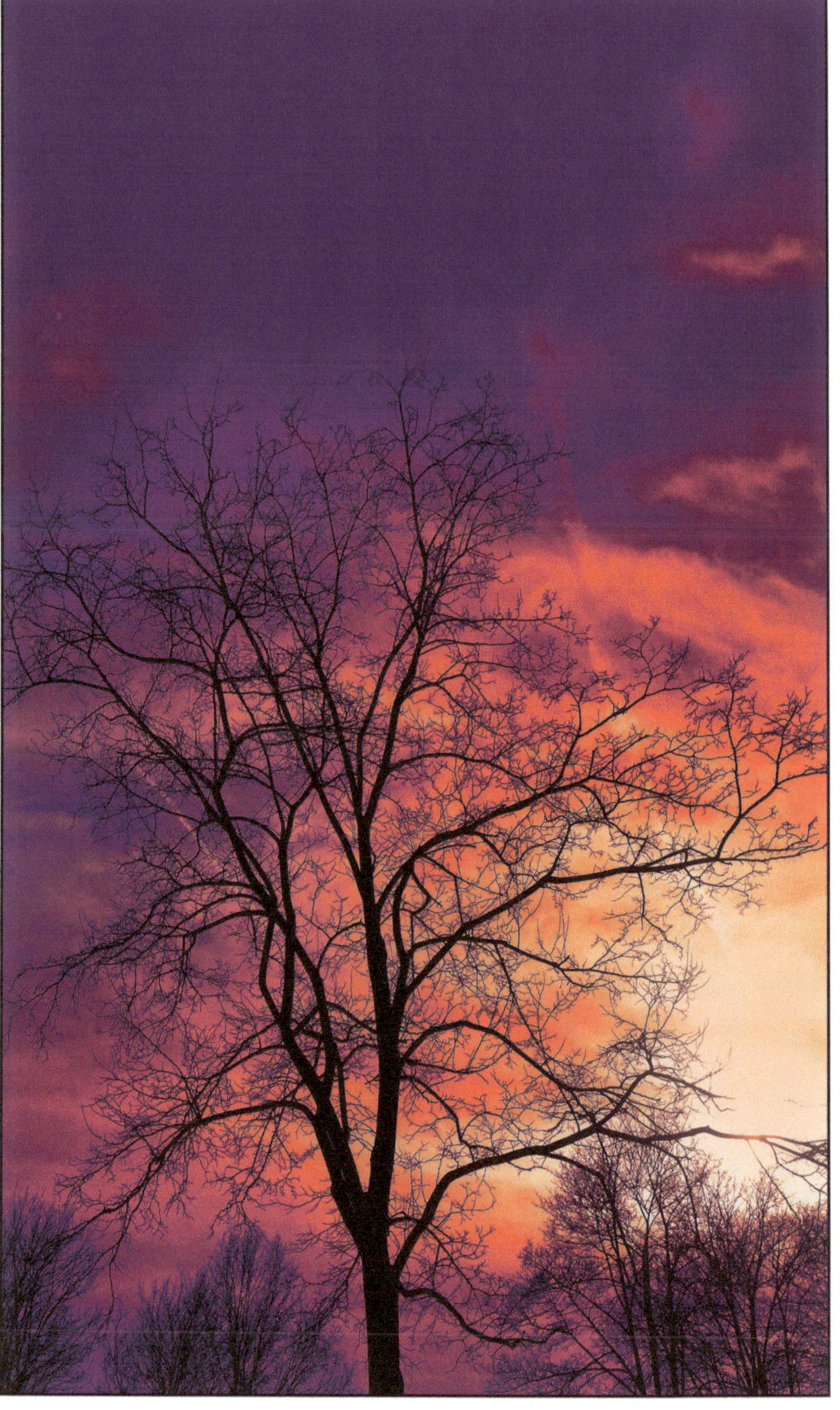

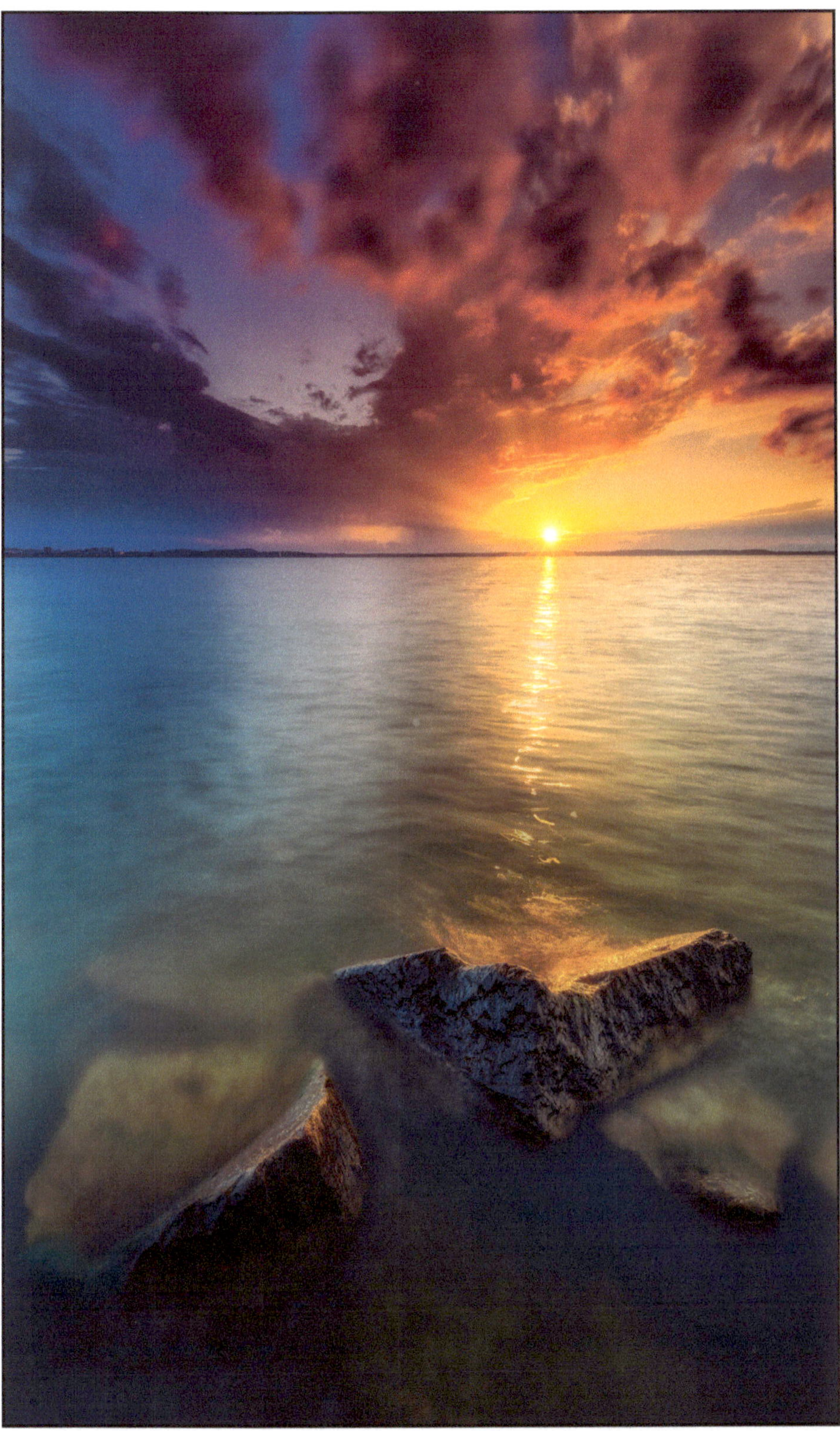

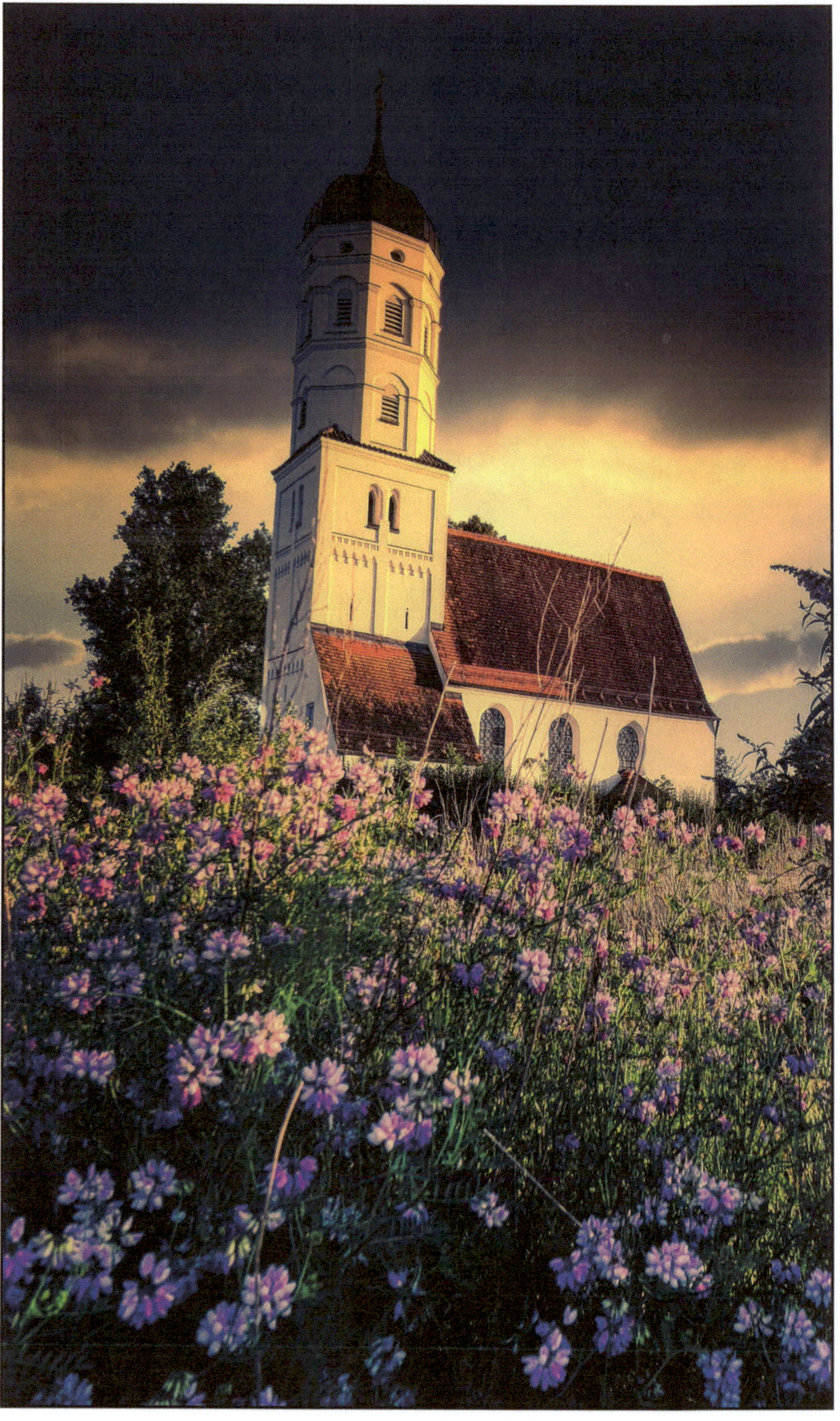

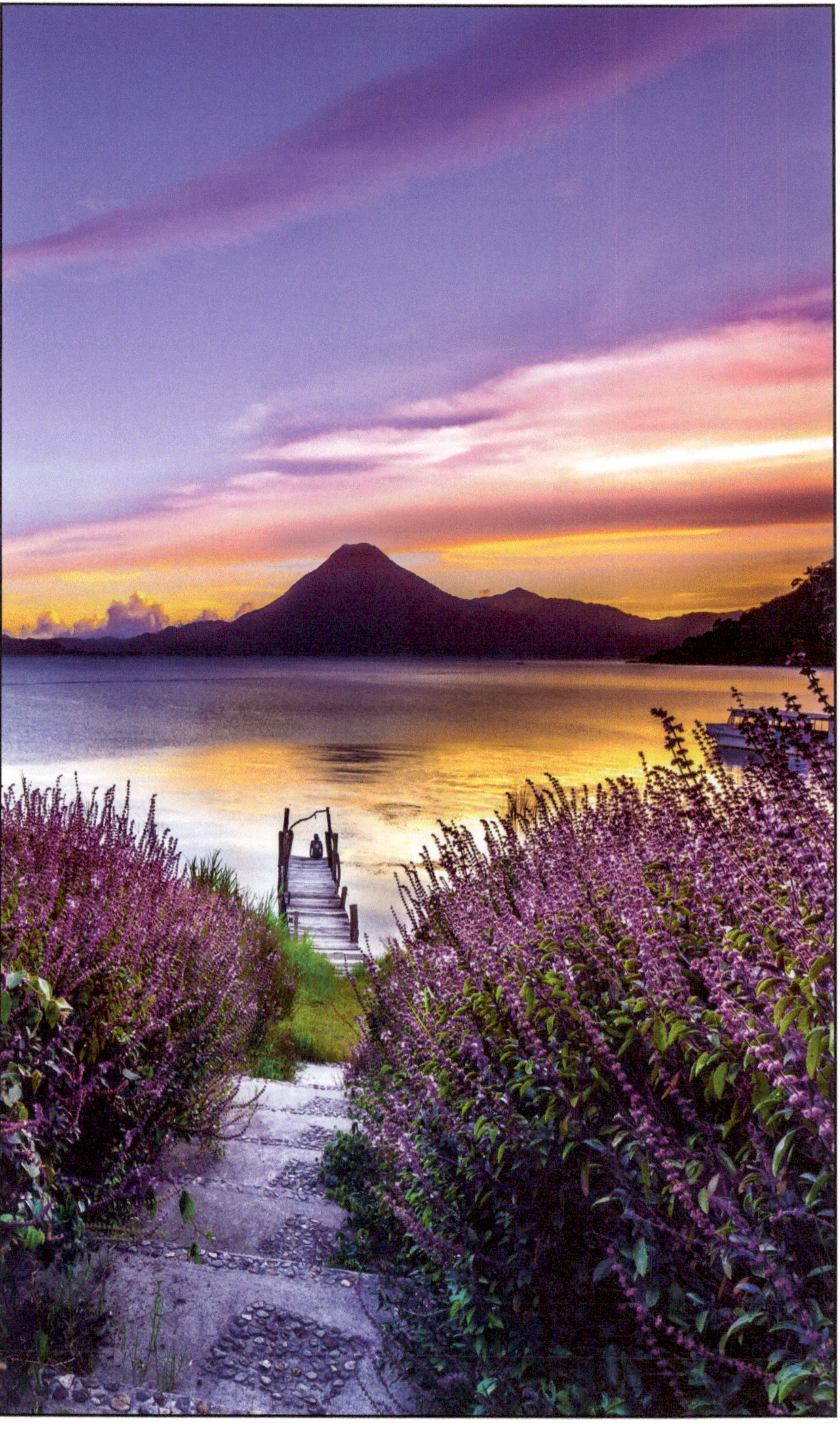

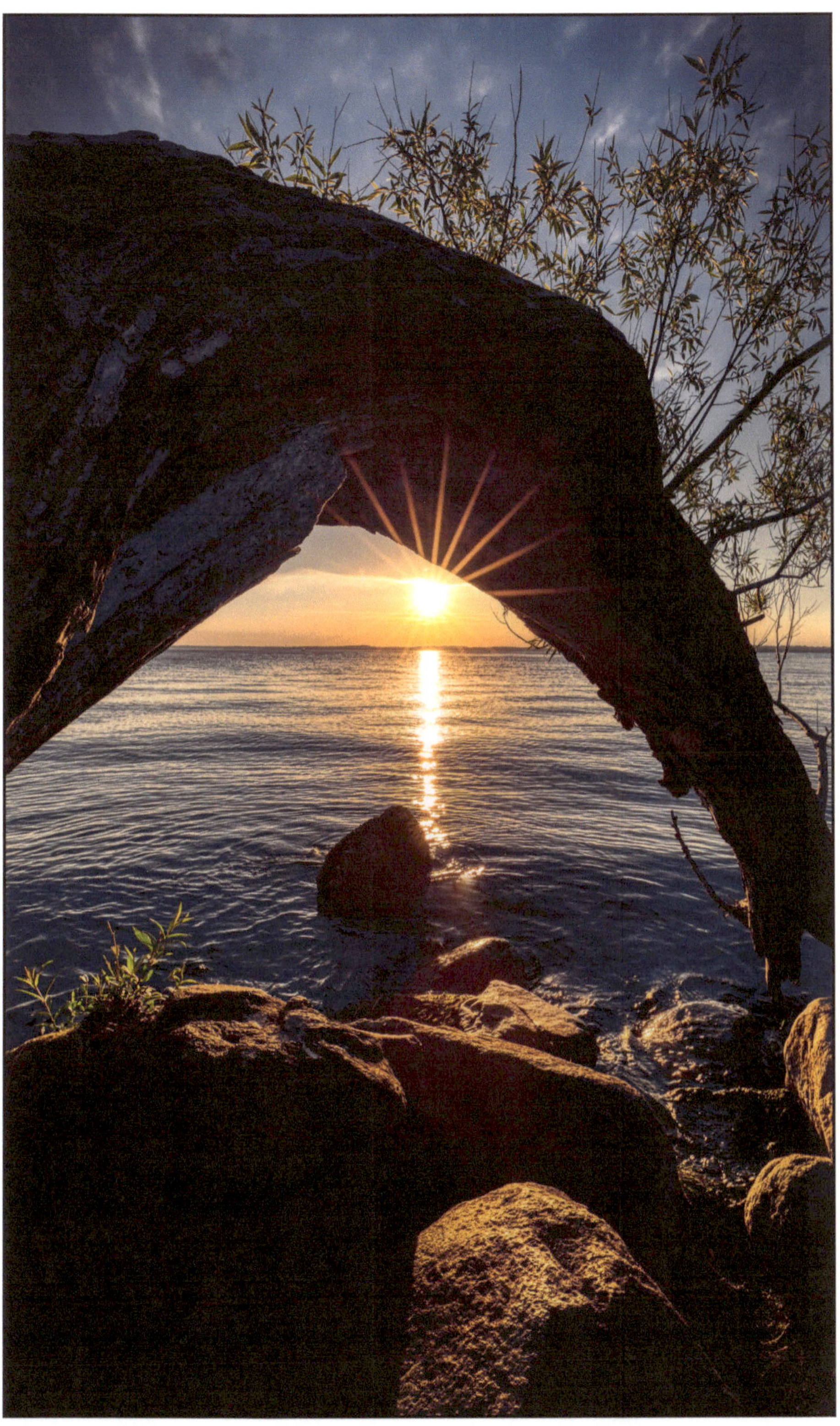

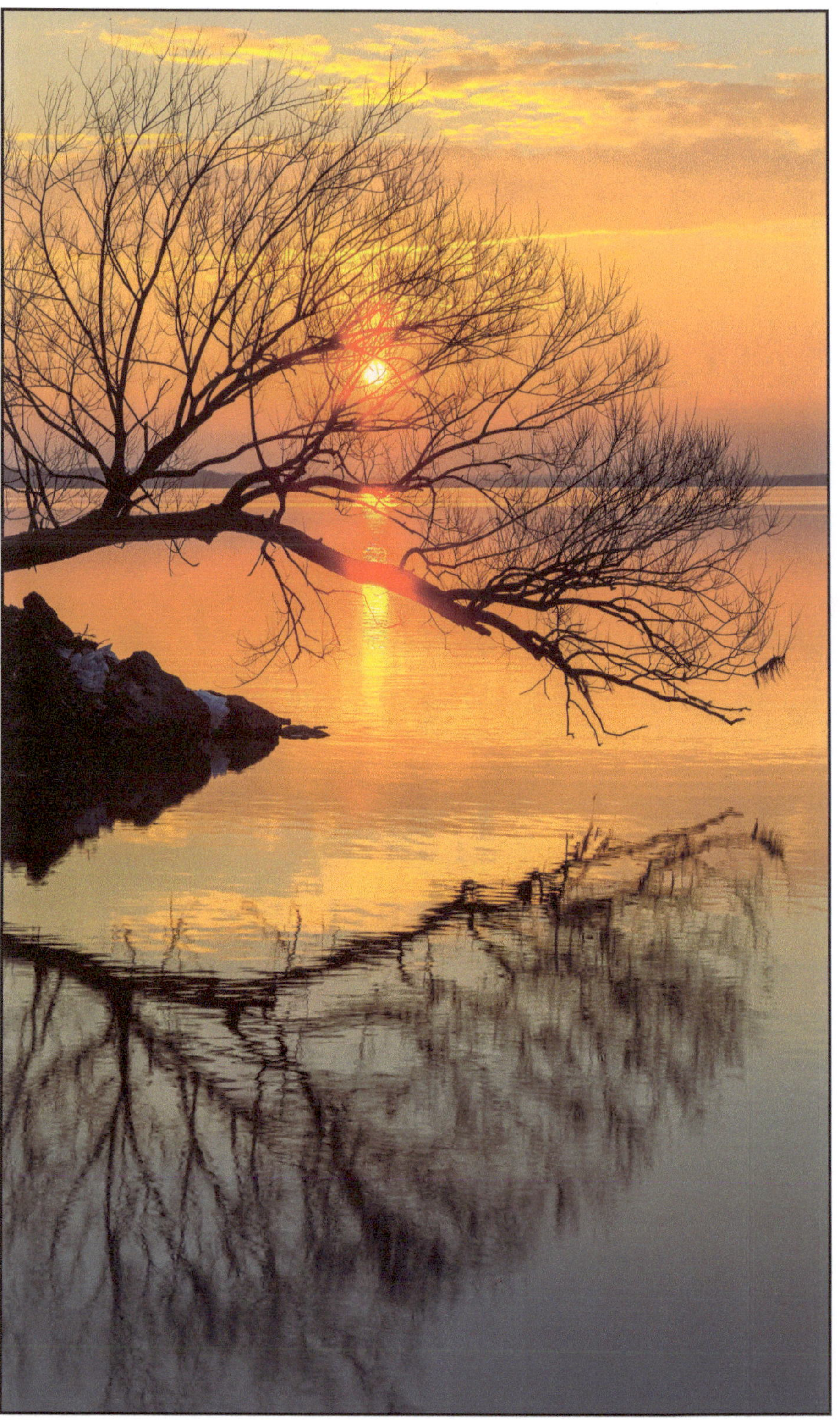

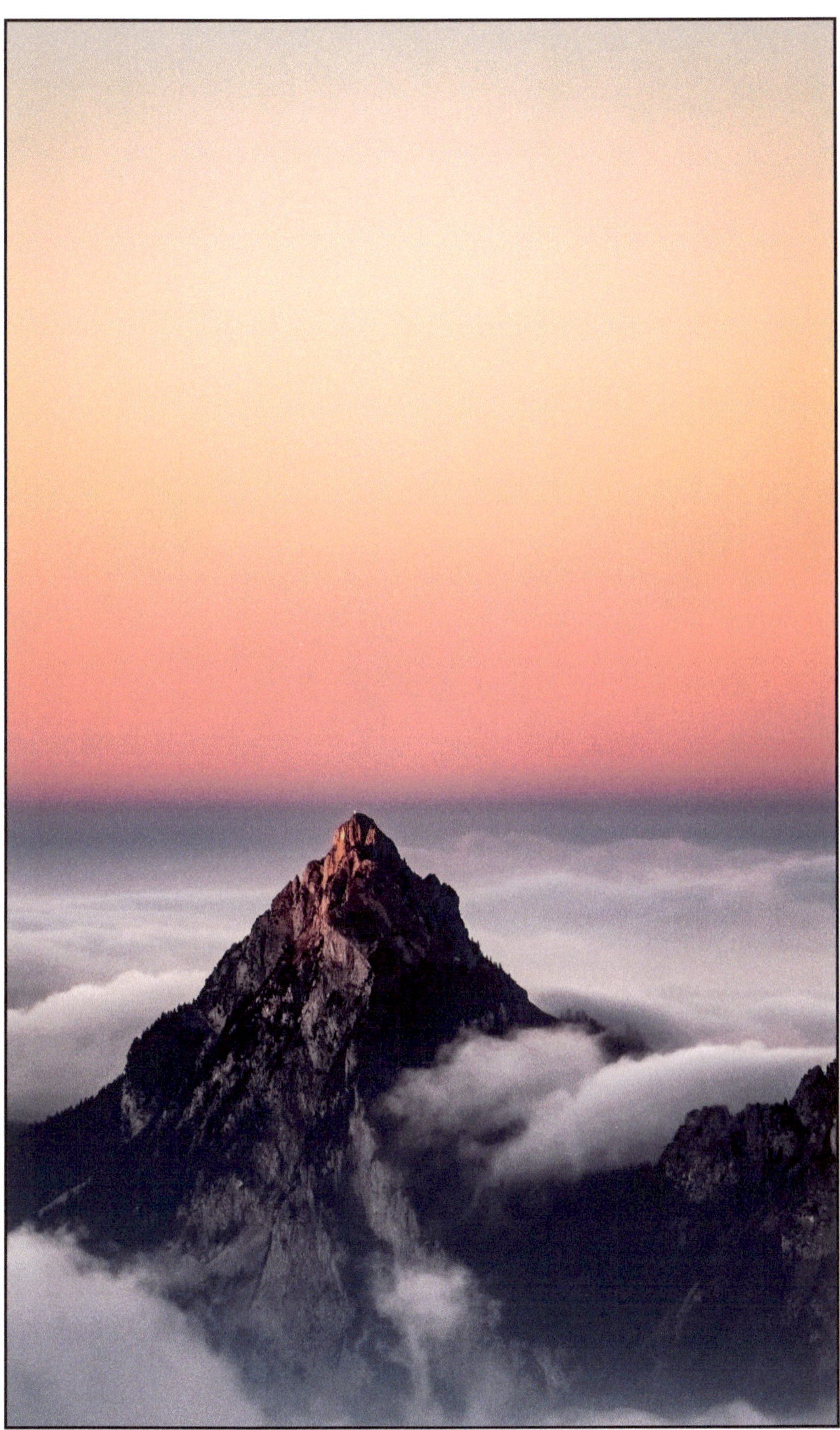

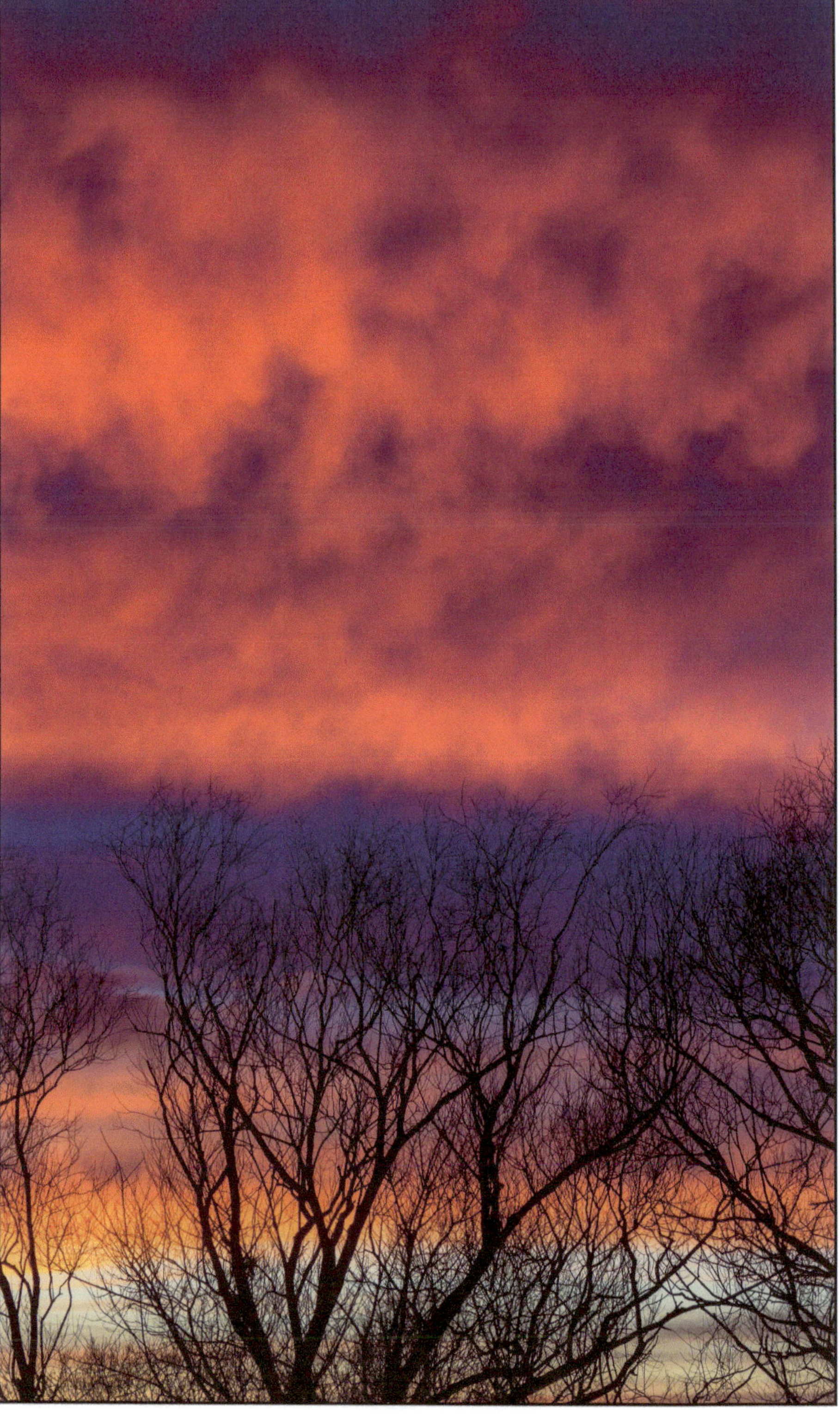

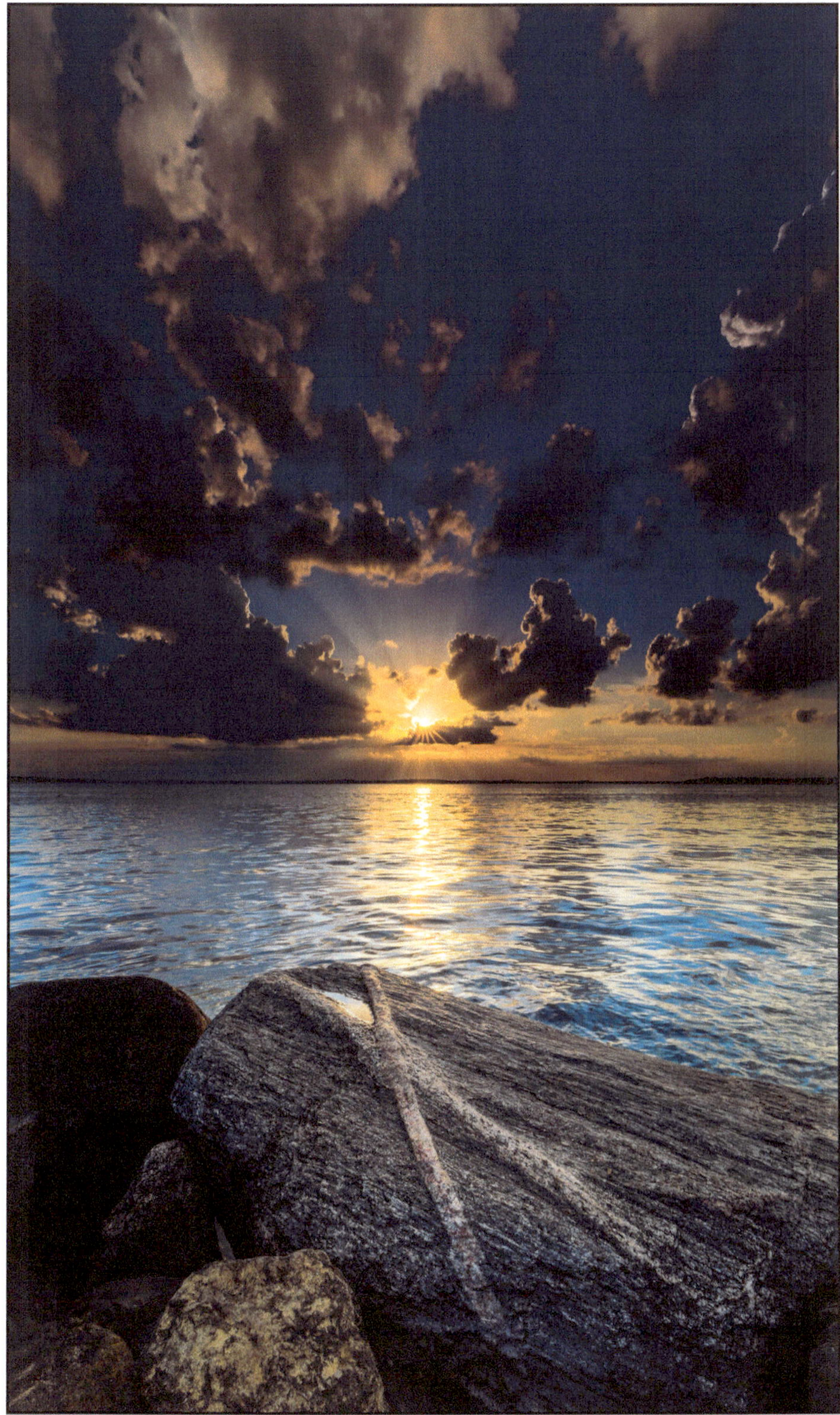